PROFESSIONS - TRAINING, EDUCATION AND DEMOGRAPHICS

THE CHAMPION IN YOU

LESSONS FROM PROFESSIONAL BOXING ABOUT HOW TO SUCCEED IN LIFE AND WORK

PROFESSIONS - TRAINING, EDUCATION AND DEMOGRAPHICS

Additional books in this series can be found on Nova's website under the Series tab.

Additional E-books in this series can be found on Nova's website under the E-book tab.

PROFESSIONS - TRAINING, EDUCATION AND DEMOGRAPHICS

THE CHAMPION IN YOU

LESSONS FROM PROFESSIONAL BOXING ABOUT HOW TO SUCCEED IN LIFE AND WORK

ROBERT J. SCHINKE

nova publishers
New York

For permission to use material from this book please contact us:
Telephone 631-231-7269; Fax 631-231-8175
Web Site: http://www.novapublishers.com

LIBRARY OF CONGRESS CATALOGING-IN-PUBLICATION DATA

The champion in you : lessons from professional boxing about how to succeed in life and work / Robert J. Schinke, editor.
p. cm.
Includes index.
ISBN 978-1-62081-612-7 (hardcover)
1. Boxing--Psychological aspects. 2. Boxers (Sports)--Psychology. I. Schinke, Robert J.
GV1133.C44 2012
796.83--dc23

2012013590

Published by Nova Science Publishers, Inc. ✝ New York

I dedicate this book to my wife Erin and two children Harrison and Pierce.
Erin, thanks for pushing me to write this book.
Harrison and Pierce, thanks for being right there at the end of each day's writing ready to play.

CONTENTS

PREFACE

I have worked with world champion boxers for fifteen years as a motivational coach. Having observed these athletes in action, one thing is apparent: their approach to boxing holds metaphors for daily life and the challenges that each one of us encounters. Take a moment and consider all that boxing movies evoke in moviegoers, and why there has been a mass appeal to boxing blockbusters such as the Rocky series, Cinderella Man and The Fighter. These movies represent trials and tribulations experienced by the everyday person, and the stories inspire persistence. We can actually see a little of ourselves, or the selves we want to be in each champion's story. Phrases like "doing battle", "delivering the knockout punch", "being a scrapper", and "being up against the ropes" are all terms that many of us use as expressions.

There are idiosyncrasies to every boxer, meaning each has certain keys to his success. Similarly, you have unique motivational practices that contribute to your performance, for better and for worse, when you encounter life's pressures. However, we also share a few common motivational practices. What we will consider in this book are the strategies we can share in common, built from the motivational practices of professional boxers. Every person is metaphorically expected to enter the ring and do battle with personal fears, insecurities, and adversaries. The question is will you battle back with a sound strategy and conviction?

Based on my experience preparing elite boxers, the strategies forthcoming reflect tactics for battle proposed for your significant life events. These life events will need to be tackled with forethought and a sound strategy. What I am about to propose in this book is divided into 16 short chapters that contribute progressively to the bottom line of performance excellence. Each step is intended to take you a little closer to a dream you might be pursuing.

Your dreams, much like the dreams of world champion boxers, require a progressive approach that makes sense, and helps you narrow your focus in a meaningful way from today, onward to the win.

There are no guarantees that you will win every battle you engage in. However, by resourcing "The Champion in You" when working through your preparation for battle, by breaking training, choosing an effective supporting cast, integrating sparing partners, employing a performance plan, and rebounding from adversity, you will significantly increase your chances of top level performance. Your wins versus losses ratio will dramatically improve, and you will become a champion with a knockout punch and the sort of ring savvy that will leave your opponents envious.

About the Author

Robert Schinke is a sport psychology professor at Laurentian University and the Canada Research Chair in Multicultural Sport and Physical Activity. Robert has worked in the world of professional championship boxing for over fifteen years. A former Canadian Equestrian Team Member and Pan American Games athlete, Robert's motivational research was awarded the 2008 Canadian Sport Science Research Award. As a motivational consultant in sport, Robert has been featured in the Globe and Mail, Ottawa Citizen, Journal de Montreal, La Presse, Radio Canada, and CTV. His consulting has also been featured on the Discovery Channel, ESPN, and during HBO World Championship Press Conferences found on YouTube. Robert is presently the Director of Professional Standards for the Association of Applied Sport Psychology – the largest global applied sport psychology association. He has published nine applied sport psychology books about various aspects of sport motivation. His research interests span cultural interventions, resilience, and athlete adaptation. When not working as an academic, or assisting professional athletes, Robert lives and plays in Sudbury, Ontario, Canada, with his wife Erin and their two children Harrison and Pierce.

Declaration

I have worked with elite amateur and professional boxers since 1996. Some of these boxers are Canadian born, and others have immigrated to Canada either as youngsters or as professionals seeking out lucrative athletic careers in North America. The content that follows in this book is built from my own experiences and perspective as a motivational consultant, constructed from a compilation of experiences across athletes.

You will also find that I have not named my former and current clients. The specifics of our work must remain confidential. I am governed by professional standards and an ethics code. Consequently, the anecdotal interpretations I share with you are anonymous and I have ensured that the trust and confidence established with each boxer's working team remains intact. Instead, you will find testimonials from people who work within the boxing world. I have come to know these people through my work, as friends. These testimonials are provided to confirm my contextual credibility, over and above my educational background.

What I propose to offer you are some transferable life lessons from successes acquired in the world of world championship professional boxing. These lessons are yours to press into action during the championship battles you choose to engage in.

TESTIMONIALS FROM THE BOXING WORLD

The major part of my success is not a secret; I am always well prepared both mentally and physically. I turned pro in 2005 right after my participation to the 2004 Athens Olympics Game and Rob was a must in my professional team. June 19, 2009 was a life-changing day for me. A lot of people doubted me but Rob encouraged me to believe in myself. I did exactly that and came home with the WBC world champion. I was the best in the world! I couldn't believe that I was world champion! I must give credit to Rob for being a big part of my success because of the mechanics that he used to help build my confidence. I am very thankful that I have had the pleasure to work with a man of this magnitude. He taught me the hard work, discipline, determination and self-confidence necessary for big wins. He can also teach you everything if you want to succeed in life. Thank you Rob! – Jean Pascal Multiple Belt World Boxing Champion.

I have worked with Rob Schinke for ten years, first with the national boxing team and more recently in elite professional boxing. Rob has become an important part of my boxers' pre-bout training camps right through to the week of the fight. The motivational strategies we've integrated in our boxers' lives can definitely transfer to you as you prepare for life's challenges and the toughest of life's opponents. Marc Ramsay – world championship boxing coach.

Robert Schinke has been an excellent resource for my elite level athletes. He has informed and motivated them to address the fundamental areas of their mental game. As a coach, working with Robert has been a very educational experience. My coaching skills have improved significantly in areas of planning, the way I communicate with my athletes, to being more observant of their behaviors both inside and outside of the ring. Muzammal Nawaz – World Champion Kick Boxer and Coach to National Team Boxers

I have always enjoyed working with Dr. Robert Schinke. My athletes liked him as well, they knew they could count on him and he never let them down. His positive attitude had a great impact on the National Team boxers and their results in the ring. Matt Mizerski – Former Technical Director and National Coaching of Canadian National Boxing Team.

It is fair to consider that the sport of high performance is subjected to very high training loads and these are growing continuously, which generates constant emotional tensions for the boxer. Without a good psychological preparation, it is virtually impossible to achieve high and stable results in contemporary sport. That is why all competitors need to train their mind. It is therefore important for a motivational consultant to be present during preparation and competition. It has been a great honor to work in our team with Dr. Robert Schinke. His high level of knowledge about sports psychology and his wise guidance to many professional fighters. Dr. Pedro Luis Diaz Benitez, former Cuban Olympic Coach and current professional boxing coach.

STEP ONE: THE FIGHT IN THE DOG

The life of a professional boxer is never easy. One of the lessons learned by professional boxers happens when there is the discovery that talent is important, but so too is effort and also one's depth of determination. If asked to choose between ability and depth of determination, I would say that determination is far more important and ability though important, is often overrated.

There is an old saying many boxing coaches have shared with me when a less talented boxer has overpowered a more talented and skilled boxer: "it is not the dog in the fight, but rather, the fight in the dog". Boxing is a sport where one boxer overcomes the other and becomes the big dog by taking the fight out of his opponent.

In life we all know people with a high level of potential and intelligence. A few of these people exert the effort and persistence in their life journey and become leaders in their professions and hopefully, also winners in their personal life. You certainly know of highly talented people in your workplace. Some of your talented co-workers will never reach their potential. Every employee hits roadblocks along the way and some become soured through the challenges they encounter.

Others tend to work quietly under the radar, gain the requisite skills, continue to work away steadily, and then slowly but steadily, rise to the top of the heap. Leaders in the workplace are often not talented in the conventional sense of being frontrunners from the very beginning.

Those who rise to the top are determined people who shatter glass ceilings and persist when others around them don't. Persistence and determination are the most important ingredients when seeking excellence. So, really, it is not the dog in the fight that's important: it's the fight in the dog!

KNOWING YOURSELF

Over the last ten years I have worked with many high quality professional boxers. I began working with elite boxers in 1996, with the Canadian National Boxing Team. I met the technical director of the team at that time, and after much pleading by me, he agreed to have me join in with a national team training camp. I was on trial with the team and watched very carefully. There were several accomplished athletes on that team. The athletes were meeting just after the 1996 Olympics to debrief and all of them knew about sport psychology, and also about being self-motivated.

The team members were sitting in a circle, and I wasn't really prepared to speak at length about "motivation", though in hindsight I should have been. Stumbling for topic matter when suddenly put on the spot, I grasped the importance of knowing oneself. Every person is a performer, and we all have certain patterns that lead to great performance and certain patterns that undermine our abilities. I asked during that discussion how many among the team systematically tracked the aspects contributing to their performance. Following my question there was stone silence. The athletes I was sitting with knew generally how to perform at the elite level – they already had at least one Olympic experience and many other international tournaments under their belt. And yet, not a single athlete systematically considered the aspects that contributed to any of his previous tournament performances. It should be acknowledged that these athletes were amateur elite athletes - not full-time professionals. As you will see in the chapters that follow, the elite among professional athletes tend to know their mind and body extremely well.

Like the professional boxer, when we have a great day at work or play, there are specific reasons that explain the "why". The reason why talent is overrated, in part, has to do with the performer's over-reliance on talent at the expense of limited self-awareness. A self-aware performer knows how much sleep is required the night before an important day's work, what meal sits well before an important morning, when to eat, how soon to arrive at the office in order to be focused and prepared for battle, and what emotion to use when going in for the kill. Without self-awareness, performance is a hit and miss phenomenon built from the bricks and mortar of guessing. The sort of confidence required for excellent performance is built from self-awareness and good decisions, derived from facts. The bottom line for each of us is that self-awareness is among the most important skill that we need to engage in when we seek excellence.

I work with very few boxers these days and the reason is that I choose my clients carefully. Concurrently, I am also a full-time professor and federal government funded academic researcher. My most successful client at present is involved in a multi-fight deal with HBO, only six fights after becoming a professional world champion in his weight division. Though I worked with the athlete in the amateurs, our work really began four years ago when the athlete's career was stalled out. When we re-committed to working together there were many briefings and debriefings after training until the athlete solidified his own unique motivational know how. Though few believed in the athlete just three short years ago, he is now highly aware, confident, and also valued as a hot commodity by the viewing public. When opponents look into my client's eyes they see someone who is self-aware: someone who is going to bring the fight to them.

How Do You Become Self-Aware?

You need to learn about the intricate aspects that make you tick. What makes you perform is unique to you, and in some ways very different from your co-worker. Each day, you need to sit down and reflect over the day's event. Take five minutes and identify one aspect in that day that either worked or did not work for you. Next, de-construct the experience and look for all of the lead-up events that eventually ended in the outcome you experienced. Consider your sleep amount, your diet, your level of exercise that day, how you were dressed, how you carried yourself in terms of posture, how you felt emotionally, and how you communicated with others. Finally, write down one sentence that becomes your life lesson gained from today. Regardless of whether the lesson is from an optimal day or one where you fell short, learning from the event makes every experience valuable. Remember, you need to discover what makes you tick and then build what you've learned into your daily life practices.

Considering What Efforts Are Required

It is never easy to choose a path toward excellence and success. There are many people who pass judgment from the sidelines. During my work with each elite boxer there were sideline commentators readily able to provide all of the reasons the client would not succeed. In many cases, sadly, the best of performers became contaminated and reduced to a smaller size of stature by the debilitative words of their detractors. People sometimes do not like excellence in others because it reminds them just how ordinary their life choices are.

For boxers, few travel the road to excellence and in fact, 99% of the money earned by professional boxers goes to less than the top 1%. These boxers are the cream of the crop, and they have a lot to offer each one of us in term of life lessons. The foundation to these lessons is hard work and commitment. It is easy enough to work hard on a given day and earn one's wages. It is an entirely different story to commit and engage at the beginning of each day, and then to follow through on that commitment every day. Success is won in the trenches, and not from a single day's efforts.

There are days in every boxer's training when life is not fun and it is a challenge to get out of bed. In fact, as I wrote this sentence, I was sitting in Bogota, Columbia with a boxer struggling to do begin his training camp. The first day I arrived he looked completely flat in emotion. By yesterday evening, three days post-arrival, he was starting coming to life, and two days later he was his old self. There is no doubt, like my client, you will also go through days that are harder to get through than others – especially when there is a hard road ahead before a battle. It is during those days that you have the opportunity to push through fatigue and engage where most others would just prefer to cruise through the day. To be among that top one percentile and earn 99% of life's rewards, you need to apply a significant amount of effort when and where others opt to take it easy and relax. Excellence is not a part-time job. Successes are accomplished from moments where others choose not to apply themselves.

So How Do You Get That Extra Effort?

Take notice on a day where you seem to be flat in energy and emotion. Where you might typically might have thrown in the towel and cruised your way through the day, do something different and re-commit yourself. Grit your teeth and really push yourself back to increased effort – like it or not. If you are sitting at your desk and no energy is flowing in relation to the challenge you are facing, stand up, move around the office, get your heart rate up, open your posture, tighten your stomach, bounce up and down, and then go on the attack. Don't give up on yourself and call it a day. Instead, do something that most people wouldn't do and start focusing on higher quality output – get moving. As you become more focused, your mind and body will react synergistically and great performance will be yours once more for the asking – on demand. As the great Muhammad Ali once said, "I hated every minute of training but I said, don't quit, suffer now and live the rest of your life as a champion". It is not easy to engage in effort each and every day, but then again, what are the consequences of opting out of that engagement? The rewards and consequences of this crucial question are yours to harvest – assuming you choose to apply yourself where others dare not.

Mobilizing Resources to Reach the Goal

There is an old chauvinist saying that "behind every great man, there is a great woman". Though you will obviously disagree that men should be in front, and women behind them, we could agree that each of us needs support in order to persist, especially when life's challenge unfold. In the world of boxing, there are several current and past world champions who somewhere along the way forgot the people who supported them onto greatness. These sorts of performers climbed and clawed their way to the top, gaining support and reassurance by those who cared for them when it was needed most. Then once at the top, they forgot who helped them along their journey, and consequently lost themselves. One well-known example of this phenomenon was Mike Tyson.

Part of readying to put up a good fight, is knowing you have the necessary resources and assistance to persist and battle your way onward to excellence and ensuing victory. For those supportive resources to be there when you need them most, you must first ensure you know who your resources are. Far too often, great support systems go unacknowledged by those in the thick of performance. Great supportive resources are people who are positive, challenging of you, consistently there when you need them most, and suggestive of sound - progressive decisions and good management.

It isn't easy to find great resources, and it is even more challenging to keep those resources mobilized and at the ready. Not long ago, I sat in a conference room with Groupe Yvon Michel, a professional boxing management team. We met with one world champion (unnamed), followed by a very promising boxing prospect. In the first meeting, it was suggested to the world champion he look very carefully at his entourage and consider re-configuring who is in his supporting cast. The champion failed to re-configure his entourage and when he was in the final days for his next fight he became a deer caught in the headlights due to a lack of effective support from his team. He was knocked out very early on in the fight, and he never rebounded from his poor decisions. Sadly, his chosen support staff were nowhere to be found after the fight as the athlete tried to pick up the pieces of his life. Success could have been the boxer's for the taking and during a crucial meeting about his career he made the wrong decision, incorrectly supported to that decision by a few people he looked to for guidance.

The second athlete decided he needed a more comprehensive level of support in order to achieve excellence. The meeting was a heated affair that eventually ended in sound decisions on the part of the boxer. As a side note, there is nothing wrong with arguing, so long as solutions are fully considered within the discussion. People are entitled to their opinions, and well-informed opinions are always useful when seeking good career decisions. For the rookie athlete, three experienced staff (me included) were hired on, and in the athletes next fight, he became world champion. This once young and inexperienced boxer now performers on HBO - each time for a lucrative pay day. He has surpassed what most every boxer achieves in the professional ranks. He earns a great living, and he has achieved a level of security in terms of his knowledge and finance that places him at the very of pinnacle of professional boxing.

The obvious difference between these two boxers just discussed was a conscious decision by each one to employ an entirely different type of team support. The fact is, we need to be challenged, we need to be held accountable, and we need the correct people surrounding us to push us upward and onward to excellence. Becoming a pugilist in your own world will not be an easy task, but even more difficult is allowing your life to slide by in a pathway that dead-ends in mediocrity. The fact is you need to be comfortable with being slightly uncomfortable. For that to happen, you need people around you who are intelligent, with keen instincts, and of equal importance, your need people who will dare to push you to the very end of yourself, where greatness resides.

Adopting a Holistic Approach to Performance

Excellence cannot just happen in the confines of the ring, or in your case, just within one aspect of your life such as a workplace. Excellence is a broader commitment toward living life to its fullest. Some people might believe, just as many boxers on the downturn believe, that living a grand life is all about "la vida loca", or partying, drinking, moving from partner to partner, and the like.

The longest standing of great performers, people such as Bernard Hopkins, are mostly comprised of those with a healthy professional life, built in part from a good diet and limited caffeine and alcohol. Also in terms of professional living, performance will rarely happen unless we have a positive work environment. To focus, you need quiet, structure, time lines, and synergy with others in the workplace. Similarly, I have witnessed one training camp in particular while an unnamed world champion trained for a mandatory defense of his world title. He and his team lacked in communication, the coach was disinterested, and the athlete was situated in a loose structure where there was a general lack of hunger and ambition. The end product of that formula was a sad - devastating loss for the athlete.

It is much easier to make it to the top of an area than to forge ahead once you are already among the cream of the crop. Young champions are energetic, focused, committed, and most often, collaborative. Those who are longstanding world champions such as a Bernard Hopkins persist in their efforts and also stay on top of their workplace environment. Having just consulted with one client as he battled on HBO against Hopkins I was astounded by just how committed this legendary fighter and his team are. Their coaches and managerial staff, more than twenty years into their team relationship, remain engaged and coordinated as the team shoots for higher and more exciting goals with each success. Bernard is forty-six years old and still going strong – as the oldest world champion boxer in history. For greatness to happen time and again, year after year, the environment has to be just right. The best of performance environments are made and then always refined, carefully crafted by the boxer and his coaching staff. You, like an outstanding boxer, need to build your environment, and unlike most people you will compete against, seek to be an active contributor and leader in your environment. You are at the center of your team.

One's personal life must also be in good shape. I know of great boxers who become vulnerable performers, not because they are unable to be athletic performers in the confines of the ring. Instead, great boxers sometimes become vulnerable because they allow their personal life to reduce them into shambles. If you are unable to go home at the end of the day and unwind, laugh, have a confidant, and live in a home that you love, you cannot be invigorated over the long-term. Far too often, striving performers, be they boxers or business professionals, focus exclusively on their workplace. At the end of the day their sole investment is found in their work, and so they forget to create a refuge where they can recharge their batteries and then live to fight another day, one day into the next, through to excellence.

To be excellent, you first need to be brutally honest with yourself. If you are excelling in both aspects of your life, the personal and the professional, you know what it feels like to be in balance and at peace. Inner turmoil happens when people cannot let go of their work life, sometimes to the point where they are attached at the hip with their wireless device and internet, deep into the evening. These sorts of achievers are not only wireless, they are also wired, and sadly, disconnected. You need to unplug and attend to your personal life. When at work, you need to be "at work" in terms of your focus, and not feeling the remorse caused by the neglect of family and friends. When at home and at play, you need to be present in that moment. There is a time and place for everything, and that is why in boxing, we speak about "living to fight another day". No boxer fights all day and all night – that is unless he is choosing to end in burnout.

Reminders from Your Corner

- Knowledge starts with self-awareness and spreads outward.
- Talent is overrated; perseverance and work ethic eventually trumps talent.
- You cannot make it on your own. You need support from colleagues, friends, and family.
- The support you build for yourself needs to be composed of intelligent – constructive team members.
- To be a performer you need a broader, balanced approach to excellence inside and outside the ring.

STEP TWO: BECOMING THE CONTENDER

At the beginning of his professional career, the high quality boxer takes on easier opponents and builds his record. For the most part, the first fifteen or so fights are not meant to be battles, they are just bouts upon which to build experience and confidence. It takes two years or so to build a record of success against easy competition before a promising boxer is ready to tackle a better than average opponent. By then, the boxer is regarded as a contender, typically with an unblemished record.

Contenders are people with lots of promise and some indicative early success. Though the term "contender" is usually referenced in relation to boxers, it is also relevant to business people, entrepreneurs and budding professionals across domains. Contenders are not born as contenders; they become contenders after a series of early wins that manifest in a winning pattern. It is virtually impossible and also unfair to over face a person with lots of promise and less experience by prematurely placing him/her in a context that is overly challenging and above one's current skill level. And yet, sadly, people are over-challenged all the time. When pushed too much, too soon, the performer becomes overwhelmed, then despondent, and then virtually helpless. One should never be pushed to the limits too soon.

The thing about contenders is they must be well managed. Their careers are built from bricks and mortar, piece-by-piece, level-by-level, step-by-step, slowly but surely. When they gain a strong foundation in their area of work, they also gain the necessary knowhow and confidence in their capacities. To be a contender, then, you need to set your sight on lofty goals, but you also require patience and a realistic timeline. Just as babies need to sit before they can crawl, crawl before they can stand, stand before they walk, and walk before they run and jump, you need to allow yourself ample time to reach professional maturation. There are important challenges you must experience, which require the necessary time to garner. Performers need to be seasoned before they engage in an epic battle. Fights need to be selected and scheduled with care, one small battle at a time, each battle chosen to hone skills, eventually required within the championship battle.

There will be a time when you gain the foundational skills and solid footing, needed to be at the top as a performer. People need to be challenged, but only through small stretches and tests each step along the way. Too much challenge all at once can stall a promising career, or lead to a short reign at the top, caused by a lack of experience. Equally, too little challenge will prevent you from really experiencing the incremental progressions needed to achieve your potential. Some people dare not test themselves, and others over-test, either too soon or too often. The middle ground of progressive challenges permit you the opportunity to become a contender, then take on, and then take down the big dogs with the skills and freshness necessary in a championship fight.

From what we discussed in Chapter One, contenders do not develop in isolation, meaning they don't materialize without help, guidance, and support from those around them. They require sage advice, solid and well-informed mentors, and good management from others in their environment. Few are the performers who become contenders without adequate support. Fewer still are the contenders who progress from hopefuls to tangible champions without a solid and well-informed entourage of people there to support and challenge. In this chapter we look closely at how to shift your thinking from a general performer's mindset to the mindset of someone clawing their way up to the top of their profession.

Choosing My Model of Excellence

So how does a boxer with dreams and aspirations decide that he wishes to embark on the journey to excellence? One of two things initially serves as the catalyst. Either the boxer views someone in his training facility that is excelling and from that observation decides to embark on his own journey to the top. Others follow boxing icons in the media and listen with care and interest as these icons reign victorious over their opponents. The model will not only be a person with lots of glitz. He will also be someone just brimming with confidence and insight, with both skills well above the standard of a typical professional.

Some models are great examples, where others showcase characteristics that sadly are not worth duplicating. A great model must be intelligent, with a keen - killer instinct, profound self-awareness, and an understanding of the ongoing work ethic required to continue his reign as king. There are other boxers who will remain nameless who become models for some, and what they profess are not good moral standards, nor contributive behaviors to excellence. Luckily for me, the champions I have worked with never were negative, dishonest, nor lazy. The best among the great champions have characteristics worthy of emulation.

In every workplace and profession there are role models worth looking considering. Sometimes we are lucky enough to be formally mentored by a model with standards of excellence. Other times we learn through acute observation of isolated characteristics such as how the champion expresses himself verbally, or how he carries himself, or how he relates with the media. To become great you really need to know where you are going and how to get there. Why reinvent the wheel? You can learn important - good lessons from the best of people around you providing you know where to look and what to emulate. When choosing your role model look for someone with a similar philosophy of life to your own, lots of integrity, smarts, and an incredible work ethic. Remember when choosing this person that great champions are systematic and extremely committed to good decisions, good strategies, and good collaborations.

The torch is eventually passed from heroes to contenders. You might well be lucky enough to learn alongside a champion and gain your fighting skills through firsthand tutelage. If you are one of the fortunate few, seize the day and gather every little tidbit of information you can. Some mentors will give generously, others will give with caution, and still others will be reluctant to share their skills at all. Just the same, if you are to be persistent as a performer, you must first begin with a thirst for knowledge, and then follow up with ongoing questions to ensure that you are correctly integrating all that you can from your mentoring.

If you have no direct access to a champion, all is not lost. The internet is a great source of information – better than most people realize. When I work with my clients, we study other champions from afar, watching their footage on YouTube and reading what they have to say to the media. From an in-depth look at the champion from afar we can gain an accurate profile of who she or he is, what that person does, and also, what her or his overall philosophy is. There is access to all kinds of information about others these days, and it is becoming relatively easy to learn from the greats without ever meeting them.

Choosing My Corner

Every great boxer has a working corner that will eventually accompany him into battle. The best of working corners is built with three to five people – three of whom are central to his performance. One person is the head coach and tactician. The head coach is really the go to person among the corner staff. When the boxer searches for pathways to success and cannot find them, the head coach is there to help him connect the dots that join blend skills with good tactics. Even if the head coach has the knowledge and experience to patch in information when it is needed most, if the boxer doesn't have enough confidence in his coach, the coach's sage advice falls on deaf ears.

The assistant coach is also a crucial member of the corner staff - meaning the staff that help guide the boxer from outside of the ropes, looking in. Boxers might only have one coach speaking to them directly. Even when that is the case, the assistant coach might see a little detail that the head coach overlooks while trying to piece together the big picture. Sometimes, I have also worked with corners where the assistant coach added in motivational words that dovetailed the head coach's technical or tactical advice and suggestions. Together, these two coaches must cover off technical content and motivation, and they must work synergistically and selflessly in the best interest of the contender.

A third important person to the team is the cut man. The cut man is there to piece the athlete back together and ensure between rounds of battle that the boxer is fit to continue. He is a "hands on" person who gets in there and does the dirty work, needed from time to time as the boxer is swollen or bloodied. Sometimes you need a little patching, and there must be a person available to help keep you together when you are spread thin, exhausted, potentially injured, and in the thick of battle.

When you look at the three central corner staff I have just described, they are parallel to the roles found in most any support network. The fact is you need a chief advisor and mentor to get in there with you and look at the big picture as you take a breather in the midst of your competitive work life. That person is there for you, helping you find your way forward onward to success, even when you are floundering in what feels like a losing battle. Your head coach has the keys to your success from the outside. He knows your skills and talents, and how to pull these out of you, when at times, you forget how to apply yourself. From his words, you can re-connect the dots of ability, training, and application, and re-impose yourself upon your opponent.

You also need the equivalent of an assistant coach to share the motivational details that blend nicely with your head coach's strategic words, guidance, and direction. The assistant coach type person can also give you the praise and support you need, when you need it most. An assistant coach has a soft shoulder and is there to motivationally prop you up and assure you of your capabilities. In boxing, you will see the assistant coach do his best work in the final few seconds before the fighter returns to battle for the next round. From the corner, the assistant coach typically yells out some meaningful words that are chosen to replenish the boxer's energy and conviction. Many years ago when one of my clients, a former world lightweight champion was exhausted during his first title bout, the assistant coach asked him to apply himself and fight for his children. The result: the athlete re-engaged in the fight and won a hard fought championship bout.

Finally, the cut man is the most under-rated person in any working corner. When something goes wrong and you are taking a beating, you need someone to patch you up. This cut man is happy to get his hands dirty, glue you back together, decrease your swellings, and then send you on your way back into battle – in one piece. Combatants fall apart during battle on many an occasion. The question is not whether a fighter will fall apart, but rather whether there is a skilled member in the team to help restore the fighter back to one functioning piece. Only in one piece does the fighter really have a fighting chance of winning the battle. Take for example a world title fight during which the aforementioned athlete dislocated his shoulder. He was in the third round against a very tough and dangerous opponent when his dislocation happened. Somehow my client finished the round and returned to his corner. It was the cut man who wrapped a towel around the fighter's shoulder and then popped it back into its socket. The outcome was a very challenging series of rounds where the boxer would return to his corner, only to be put back together – literally. In the end my client retained his world title – primarily due to the cutman's ability to re-package the boxer several times throughout the battle. What followed was praise from the media and an HBO contract for his next fight.

Hand Picking My Opponents

In boxing, the selection of each opponent is an important part of how the athlete builds his fight record. I have seen quite often, boxers rushed forward to face opponents who were above their current skill level and capacities. In these instances, the boxer discovered his current limitations and far too early in his career, hit bottom in terms of his mental and physical fortitude. For athletes over faced too early on, often there is a dip in performance, a loss of confidence, and the formal stalling out of a career.

Many a boxer never recovers from poor management and being over faced by too challenging an opponent, too early in a career.

At the opposite end of the continuum, some boxers are held back far too long to the point where they never realize just how good they are. In the sport of boxing, I like to refer to such athletes as backyard performers. They stay in their comfort zone, and under the guidance of their staff, tend to seek out easier opponents so as to protect their winning record. Though a great boxer's career must be built with care and a progressive selection of opponents, those who choose to continue with a developmental level of opponents find themselves stagnating, and more often than not, they cannot even explain why their confidence is not building despite a high rate of wins. The reality is that confidence is built by stretching oneself and then succeeding, not by winning easy fights against unworthy or aged out opponents.

When a boxer is well managed, he will experience likely about twelve to fifteen easy opponents so that he banks rounds of battle and some foundational experience. Some opponents can be stopped early, and with others, he gains experience by "going rounds" and learning how to work through fatigue. If he were to always win through very quick successes, he would never learn how to battle through challenges that take more time.

The objective at a certain point, then, is to have the boxer bank lots of rounds, eventually against opponents with stamina, but during these early fights, with at least a little less skill than the contender. Some successes happen quickly and some require time and patience. The contender needs both sorts of experiences before he will ever achieve champion's status.

So, how does the strategic choosing of opponents relate to you? You need to gain your footing in your profession. To build confidence and maintain conviction, you need to decide with some careful guidance from your coaching staff what are reasonable tests of your present ability. You need to learn how to press your foot on the accelerator and slowly, gain comfort driving at progressively faster speeds for longer periods of time.

With time, you will end up stretching a little more through each progressive work or life battle. The thing is that you need to stretch a little at a time, no more, no less.

PROFILING THE ENEMY

When I began to work in boxing, I watched with interest as the head coach of the management group I worked for would sit down with his athletes and watch video footage of their opponents. By eyeballing the opponent's tendencies within the fight, the coach and athlete would work on punching combinations, footwork, body movement, and head movement to nullify the opponent's strengths and capitalize on his weaknesses. In one particular case, I sat with the coach and his athlete as they prepared for the athlete's first ever world championship bout against a very tough opponent. During the sit down meeting, the coach's objective was to show the boxer how his opponent's dangerous knockout percentages could be nullified through footwork and intelligence. These sorts of meetings are what great coaches do with their up and coming champions.

Initially, I didn't say much when boxing coaches and their athletes studied opponents. More than ten years into my practice with professional boxers, I now help to employ a much more elaborate profile of the opponent. Boxers have stylistic tendencies in the way they fight. In addition, they have psychological tactics that they try to employ to wear down opponents. As I initially wrote this paragraph, my highest profile client was readying to fight one of the masters of psychological warfare – Bernard Hopkins. Hopkins is intentionally erratic in the way he treats his opponents. I am sure you know the type of person I am referring to. These are the sorts of people whom most people feel high levels of anxiety around because they never know which personality is going to show-up for the meeting. Hopkins is crafty in the way he is able to keep his opponents and their working teams off balance.

And so, for that fight my job was to look into Hopkins' personality and tendencies through all kinds of information available through web access. I looked for consistencies in Hopkins behaviors so my client and his staff learned about the enemy, and what they could expect. This sort of tactic has won us quite a few memorable fights on the world stage, where odds makers in Las Vegas often held us at four to one odds against my client. During the lead up to that first fight, Hopkins was heard commenting that never had he experienced such a highly responsive tactical opponent in a lead-up to any of the more than fifty fights he engaged in as a two decade world champion.

There is nothing better than knowing your opponent, cold. I have already admitted you need to know yourself, but you also must know the challenges that are ahead. You need to study your opponents and know exactly where they are coming from and then, what they are seeking to do next through their pre-fight tactics. Though you likely won't be profiling the sorts of people I do, where lots of information is out there in the media, there are many ways to really prepare for your battles. You can look them up your opponents on the web and seek access to their social networking pages. You might also attempt to learn from people who know the opponent, his/her tendencies, and also the sorts of tactics that person uses. Information is power, and the best of contenders gain as much information as they can about their opponents. The objective is to know oneself and also the opponent – both people extremely well.

Now, when I refer to profiling opponents, the concept of an opponent can take on several different meanings. You might be a real estate mogul who does battle with other moguls to gain the best deals and pieces of land. You might also be someone who is getting ready for the most important job interview of your life. The opponent for you might well be an interview, and related, the people asking the interview questions. You need to know where each and every opponent is going with her or his questions. The fact is that you need to understand the context you are seeking to perform in. If you have that knowledge, in keeping with Sun Tzu's Art of War, more than half of the battle is already won, before the battle is ever fought.

Selecting Suitable Spar Partners

Before we depart for training camp and the preparation for battle, one of the important decisions made by the head coach and boxer is who should be invited to attend as a spar partner. As fights become more important there are usually two or even three carefully selected spar partners to help the boxer hone his skills in advance of the big fight.

The people chosen to fill the role of spar partner are hand picked because they bring relevant skills to the table in relation to the next opponent. One of the central skills is the ability to support the boxer, meaning the spar partner needs to be a good team player. The second core characteristic is that the spar partner must have a certain style in the way he does battle. That style needs to match and parallel the style of the boxer's upcoming opponent.

With the interpersonal and technical skills of good spar partners, the boxer will be pushed when he begins his formal training camp. The spar partner helps the boxer learn and anticipate the questions that will eventually be encountered when he steps into the ring and engages in battle. With finely tuned skills for the fight, the boxer is not over faced or caught by surprise. Again, I will say that wars are often won before they are ever fought.

People need to be challenged as I have said previously. What I didn't say was the challenges have to be built in relation to where you are going. On the job, there will be specific challenges encountered during each step on your way to the summit. Some of the challenges are foreseeable. Your job is to find one or a few spar partners who will challenge you and put you through your paces so that your next challenge is not foreign to you when you encounter it for real in the ring.

There are several ways to choose a spar partner. The worst way to choose that person is because they are easily accessible. I have witnessed world-class boxers commit that very same error. Some boxers choose their spar partners because a comfortable relationship exists amongst the contender and the spar partner. When you are seeking the right person for the role of spar partner, you need someone who is challenging; who accurately provides and foreshadows the speed bumps ahead. Finally, some like spar partners who make them look good. The job of the spar partner is to hone your skills so that you look good, when looking good is important – in the heat of battle.

Preparing My Battle Plan

The average professional boxer builds his battle plan based on generalities and often, over-simplification. Even when I watch some boxers and their corners performing during globally televised events, I am sometimes amazed by how superficial their preparation is before they go into battle. All I have to do is listen to the athletes speak in advance of the bout and then listen to the corner try to work with the athlete in between rounds. They tend to be uncertain, disorganized, and wilted, especially within those final few hours before battle. Fighters need to maintain and even build their confidence in those final few days, hours, and minutes before the bout. Those who shrink in confidence become a lesser boxer in the fight that follows. The boxer's response is merely a reflection of fight or flight.

There are two general reasons why boxers and their staff are caught by surprise. One reason is because they just don't have the know how to package together a performance plan that is built with all of the aspects needed to nullify the opponent's skills. The second reason is much more troubling: sheer laziness. Luckily, both of these reasons for potential under performance can be remedied with education and the sort of spadework in the trenches that can go into the construction of a great performance.

The sort of battle plans I like to help my team build include much more than anticipation of what each opponent is going to bring to the table. They must also integrate what my contenders need to do in advance of the chosen bout so he could place all of his ducks in a row. The things we consider include aspects of strategy, but also the needed ingredients that have to happen in advance of the fight.

Things like quantity of sleep before battle, nutrition, hydration, exercise, the correct equipment and clothing, privacy from the public, and ample time for a correctly structured warm-up. Boxers cannot go into battle fatigued, hungry, thirsty, or mentally and physically cold, nor overheated. All of the conditions need to be just right for excellence to result in the ring.

Most people go into battles with only a general understanding of what lies ahead. Being unprepared is thoroughly unnecessary 99% of the time. Every now again we will be caught off guard by a surprise uncontrollable factor, but even then, good developmental processes like the ones already discussed in relation to yourself and your opponent will arm you with the necessary skills to pull through most every unforeseen circumstance. More often than not, good preparation covers you from surprises. The thing is, you need to prepare yourself with the equal level of detail to the clients I have worked with in elite boxing. You may not be a contender in boxing, but you are a contender just the same! To contend you need to treat yourself like a valuable commodity. You need to eat well, rest well, exercise, dress well, and the like. If you don't look and feel great you aren't going to perform at your best – not even close.

Your plan extends beyond you in isolation, to you in relation to your team and the task ahead. You need to understand the challenge, why it is a challenge, and then, how to overcome it. You deserve the opportunity to excel in your performance life. But, for you to excel, you need to build a battle plan that matches with the challenge ahead. Also, remember that as challenges change, so too do battle plans. No two battle plans are the same. Equally, no two opponents are identical.

As well, plans are dynamic and should refine as you go deeper into your preparation for battle. Through effective preparation you will learn more about yourself and the challenge ahead. As your preparation refines, your confidence will also build exponentially. Push yourself, study hard in relation to this opponent, take care of yourself, and then you will be ready when the bell sounds for round one and each round that follows.

Reminders from Your Corner

- Find yourself a role model and study what that person does extremely well. No need to reinvent the wheel. Sometimes the answers are right in front of you – if only you would look in the right place.
- Build a corner around you with people who are able to balance the abilities of technical expertise, motivation, and fight maintenance from a cut man.
- Choose your next opponent so that you stretch, and at the same time are able to overcome the challenges of the opponent.
- Pick the correct spar partners in relation to your next challenge. Remember that good characteristics of spar partners include the match of their technical skills with your next opponent, though also their willingness to be a member of your working team.

STEP THREE: BLOOD, SWEAT AND TEARS

Nothing worthwhile in life comes easy. Ask any boxer at the top of the sport and you will hear that greatness comes from blood, sweat and tears. There are lots of professional boxers out there and most of them are journeymen. They are generally speaking professional boxers, and yet most hold down a part-time job to subsidize their athletic dreams and ambitions.

The sad thing is few boxers can really squeeze out a living in boxing, and as a result, many do not invest the necessary time and effort to become great – they just don't have the time and freedom to achieve greatness. Among those who reach the summit as professional boxers, most commit fully to the task of training and bout preparation from very early on in their career. Life for such athletes is not easy at the best of times. However, their life does become progressively easier because of good decisions made early on during hard financial times. The decision to engage in full-time training eventually becomes the tipping point in their favor a year or two into a boxing career, when purses for fights can really start to pay off.

I have never heard of a great boxer who has not struggled and nearly starved early on in their career. The hard times are not just about dollars and cents. They also relate to the physical challenges associated with each day's training as young boxers seek to evolve into hardened fighters. For those who make it to the top, these athletes invest their lifeblood very early on and suffer through the most grueling of training. One of the most amazing boxing coaches I work with is Pedro Diaz, a former amateur boxing coach – a man involved in the development of over twenty Olympic boxing champions. When Pedro trains a boxer, he has them do all kinds of grueling things. One of the most challenging exercises he asks is for his athletes to climb up a rope with their bare hands. Within the first few attempts, every boxer suffers rope significant burn. The skin from their hands is literally left on the rope.

The hardships experienced by developing boxers is physically brutal and not for the faint of heart. Recently, a highly promising unnamed contender that I know relatively well hit a speed bump in his progression to the top. The boxer was undefeated with almost every one of his wins achieved by knock out. The boxer had to fight a world title eliminator and if he won that fight, the next fight would have been for a world title, televised on HBO. The boxer was one fight away from becoming a multi-millionaire. He was so close to success that he and his team could taste it. The athlete was not my client and from afar I had my reservations about whether he had the focus to really make it. He ate a ridiculous diet, his weight often ballooned well above what it should be in between fights, he dated serial partners, and for certain, his life was not fully committed to the blood, sweat and tears work ethic needed to make it as a boxing contender.

The first few rounds of the fight saw the young pugilist dominating his opponent. He was show boating, sticking out his tongue, beating up on the opponent, and assuming that the fight would be another easy bout for him. The opponent took his lumps, was patient, and waited to take the young buck deeper into the fight where blood, sweat and tears would become the factor separating the winner from the loser. By the end of the fifth round the young contender was getting hit, his face became swollen and before long he had a bloodied nose. By the sixth round the more experienced and composed opponent started to press ahead and won his first round. Half way through the seventh round the opponent connected with an accurate shot that reached behind the guard of the young boxer and sent him to the canvass for the first time ever in his career. From then on, the young boxer never gained his footing. Sadly, the bout was stopped a minute or so later. The young boxer missed his multi-million dollar payday by one fight. He was so close to making it.

Success from failure is always differentiated in terms of inches - an inch here and an inch there. Before you know it, two equally talented athletes can be miles apart in terms of their skills, professional records, and financial opportunities. Though the young boxer was talented and everything on paper suggested that he would make it, the one thing he lacked was a willingness to invest in his preparation through blood, sweat and tears. There are times when things just don't come easy, and for that matter, greatness never comes easy. As Muhammad Ali recognized: "The fight is won or lost far away from witnesses—behind the lines, in the gym, and out there on the road, long before I dance under those lights". You have to invest in yourself each and every day. Each day is an investment in you, much the same as one who puts a dollar into a piggy bank, daily. A dollar has little value, but if you invest one dollar each day for a few years and also factor in the compound interest, in a few years you will have saved quite an amount of currency. The young boxer was caught up short, but his setback began well in advance of the loss; it's just that he had yet to pay the price for his poor investment strategy. In this chapter we will speak about the hardship and investment you need to commit throughout your career, that in turn will lead you to contender's status.

Being Comfortable with the Uncomfortable

Not long ago I went off to a training camp with an anonymous client who is a world-renowned boxer. The first four weeks of his training were in Bogota, Columbia. What makes Bogota so unique is that it is over 8000 feet above sea level. The air is really thin at 8000 feet, I'll tell you that! The first night I was there, I went to the washroom and all of a sudden it seemed that the floor came toward me - I was blacking out. A few seconds later I got to my knees, crawled back to my bed and slept off the lack of oxygen that my brain and body craved. The air is definitely thin at the top of the world. To build a world champion sometimes we need to travel to the top of mountains where the training is most severe.

It is extremely uncomfortable training for the first week or so when you are in a high altitude situation. About five days into the camp we traveled three hours inward from Bogota to the city of Boyaca, where the altitude is 10000 feet above sea level. That day's training was grueling to watch, as the coach and I gasped for air, watching the athlete from the sideline. The athlete forged ahead. The fact is there are several benefits to pushing oneself through a challenging training environment. One gain is a physiological dividend when you learn to physically push through fatigue and exhaustion barriers before an epic fight. By pushing through exhaustion, you gain confidence in your body and its ability to weather all kinds of barriers that would screen out people who train without discomfort.

There is also a psychological dividend achieved by working through discomfort. Just as your body learns to adjust to the stressors you experience as you put yourself through paces, so does your mind. People need to learn to think on the spot and claw their way through a challenge by investing effort and focus where others just give up. When you decide to work through hardship and then battle through the challenge, you become mentally tougher. The goal is to become brutally tough on your mind and body before the battle.

If you can walk through walls in advance of the battle, what do you think you will revert to in the heat of battle? We always fall back and rely on our preparation, meaning the things that are automated and programmed into us. Evander Holyfield once stated: "A champion shows who he is by what he does when he's tested. When a person gets up and says 'I can still do it', he's a champion."

On the other hand, if you train in comfort, much like the young contender I spoke about in the last section, when discomfort starts to creep into your challenge, you won't have the knowledge, readiness, and confidence to work through it. Sometimes the light at the end of the tunnel is very far off in the distance and all you could see is a pinprick of light. In those moments, you need to continue moving forward, placing one foot in front of the other. Before you know it, that pinprick of light becomes a spot, and the spot then becomes progressively larger until you are covered by sunshine.

The reality is that you need to become comfortable with being uncomfortable. You need to learn to be willing and able to go without sleep, food, oxygen, and all of the other sorts of things that most people are unwilling to go without. You need to become a hardened competitor who attacks a challenge in the most grueling of moments and in those moments, applies intensity where others would back away. Success at the top level is for the most hardened of fighters.

Taking a Complete Approach to Fitness

Fitness and being physically prepared for battle is about lots of little decisions that compound into the larger balance sheet of whether you are ready or not to do battle. Good decisions are taken in small bite size pieces. Not long ago I worked for a company by the name of Interbox with a large stable of professional boxers. One morning I joined the coach early for a morning workout. He and I sipped our coffees while watching the boxers run their warm-up laps before training began in earnest. One boxer consistently cut a few feet of distance on each turn of the running track, and in so doing he likely saved about forty feet of distance during each lap. He believed that a snip here and a snip there in distance would save him from fatigue. Others ran the correct path on the track, and only one athlete really exerted himself fully during that training session.

We are now several years after that day's training and you could only guess what the outcome is for the dozen or so professional fighters I witnessed that morning. You guessed it: the only athlete who made it to the summit is the boxer who engaged fully in his physical training. None of the others boxers ever made it to the pinnacle as boxers. Instead these athletes, some having taken shortcuts in their training, now have much less of a financial and professional future than the one diligent athlete. There are no shortcuts to the top and if you wish to stay at the top, you need to keep investing in yourself through blood, sweat and tears.

Fitness is more than just hard training. I keep going back to the young boxer who was blown out just one fight away from a world title. He was a workhorse in the gym. Every time I would comment to his working team about his questionable focus they would all respond in tandem: "but he is an animal when it comes to training". In the back of my mind I always knew that being committed is much more than just what happens in the confines of the gym. Commitment is as much about what happens when the boxer leaves the gym as it is about what happens inside the ropes.

Fitness means looking after your body, period! You need to watch what you eat, and I don't just mean watching your weight. What you eat and drink becomes the quality of fuel that you burn as you progress through each day. If you fill your body with high-octane fuel, you have much more energy than you might have with regular octane fuel. People who fill their cars with poor quality fuel eventually hear pings and rattles from their car's motor. Also, their motors don't last as long, and mechanical maintenance is required much sooner. You are indeed what you eat and what you drink. Pure, clean food and water are needed so that you can push your body to the max every day. We ask a lot of our body each day just putting it through its paces. Don't compound the task by adding nutritional impurities – choose your fuels wisely.

Mentally, you also need to nourish yourself with care. You need to fuel your mind with constructive thinking, and solution-oriented support from others. The things that need to anchor your thinking should include "how to", "what next", and those sorts of progressive questions. As George Foreman once stated: "That's my gift. I let that negativity roll off me like water off a duck's back. If it's not positive, I didn't hear it. If you can overcome that, fights are easy." Even in the most challenging of moments, you need to continue stepping forward and nourishing your mind with constructive thoughts and a persist search for solutions to daily challenges.

In any workplace you will find at least four types of employees I've heard referred to as the four W's: (1) weasels, (2) whiners, (3) workers, and (4) warriors. Weasels try to manipulate the truth and deceive those around them through a misrepresentation of the facts. Whiners go out on their coffee breaks and complain about their work environment. I will bet that in your workplace there are a few whiners. If you are not a whiner, when you stand around these people just for a few minutes, you start to feel tension in your body and your mind. You might also start turning your focus to all of the injustices found in your workplace. Workers are people who put their nose to the grindstone, mind their own business, invest themselves in their career, and work with diligence. Workers over the long-term always trump weasels and whiners. The reason workers forge ahead over the long haul is because they fuel their minds with a forward oriented focus. Finally, warriors are metaphorically associated with those who go to war, including boxers. These people are known for their willingness to push beyond all physical and mental boundaries so that they can engage in battles and conquer new territories. Expansion is what the contender looks to do through training and the successes over a progressive list of opponents. You are a warrior and you need to conquer uncharted territory in order to fully develop.

Each Day's Commitment to Complete Training

Ricky Marciano once said: "To win takes a complete commitment of mind and body. When you can't make that commitment, they don't call you a champion anymore". It is easy to give your all on a single day. All you need to do is wake up and decide to engage. Attacking your day requires focus, energy and commitment to what lies in front of you. Then you march forward and move from one task to the next with vibrant energy. Blood, sweat and tears as a phrase suggests that people need to engage each and every day with the world around them in order to eventually reach the summit. Excellence and engagement is a day in and day out commitment.

The commitment to engagement during training begins long before the boxer ever physically walks into the gym. The decision to apply oneself completely happens when the boxer wakes up in the morning. What awaits is that day's training, and from it, another step forward toward his ultimate goal of reaching the summit as a boxer. Every little decision each day is informed by the goal of being a champion, with all that separates the athlete from his championship title being days of commitment and the inevitability of time.

By the time the boxer walks into the gym, he is on a mission. Focus narrows and there is a specific new skill or recurring weakness to be targeted that day. At the end of the day's training, many a robotic athlete will have banked more hours in the gym, but those hours will have only furthered them on a course toward becoming gym rats. The contender, on the other hand, will have worked with a purpose, bound to an overall vision.

Time must always be fully invested in the task of training and refinement. Consider the people who work, live and breath around you each and every day. How many of these people just coast through their days and choose not to invest themselves fully into the various parts that comprise their professional life? Far too many people coast through life without much thought in advance in terms of what they would like to achieve that day. We need to know where we are going in order to get there. Anything less than a healthy decision at each and every crossroad will only delay us in our pursuit of excellence.

Few are the boxers who actually make all of the right decisions in their training and their life. Equally few are the people around us who decide to take care of themselves and construct a life process that places more assets than deficits on their balance sheet. Those who live with short-term ambitions will not make sound life decisions. Each day is filled with many crossroads. Each crossroad is an opportunity to make a good decision where you can invest in yourself or a poor decision where you chip away at your advancement. I have seen many promising contenders chip away at their potential only to find out that they squandered their future.

Knowing all the decisions one has chosen in terms of training and life match with excellence is a very potent elixir for the contender. It is not enough to believe in training, he must also believe all parts of his life are well thought out so he is fully aligned with a trajectory that ends with excellence in the ring. Blood, sweat and tears is not a part-time viewpoint – it is all encompassing. You need to approach your life as if every decision you make will take you one step closer to your goal of performance excellence. Commit to yourself and bring all parts of your life into alignment with your overall objective of performance excellence.

Reminders from Your Corner

- Being fit means a lot more than most people think it does. Physical fitness means that you exercise every day and push yourself to your limits, that you sleep enough hours each night, that you eat right, and that you have time to relax and regenerate.
- Fitness also pertains to the mental (i.e. thinking) part of your life. The mental part implies that you need to be focused on constructive thinking and the knowledge of where you are going.

- Many people regard discomfort as a bad thing, but that assumption is inaccurate. People need to experience some discomfort each day in order to stretch themselves. You need to push yourself out of the comfort zone intentionally. Then when a real challenge comes your way, you will embrace the discomfort and respond by attacking the problem.
- Each day, you must be focused on your professional development. You need to consider and appreciate how today's decision contributes to the overall objective of becoming a champion.

Step Four: Talking the Talk

Chances are you have heard the saying "talk is cheap". Sometimes, when people claim they are going to go to the next level and seek excellence, those around them use the term talk is cheap to indicate that words hold little value. Other terms like "big talker" and "braggart" suggest in today's society that people should not talk large and think large.

For some years I worked in a large academic institution. Like many workplaces, the organization was built with the average performer in mind. Many people in such contexts are small talkers, and also small thinkers. Likely these people are socialized into their role as minions, or widgets.

Boxers are no different. Many, as a result of socialization, don't give enough thought and discussion to where they are going. Each time I walk into a boxing gym, I don't focus on any individual athlete. Instead, I listen to the discussions that percolate within the gym's confines. Some complain about aches and pains, others speak about fatigue, still others speak about dates and drinking, and few really discuss things relevant to that day's training. I always wonder how are these boxers building focus for the training to come that day? Many talk, but what they have to say is not pertinent to their training.

What the boxer says matters a great deal. Every word that comes out of his mouth holds some sort of value that will bring him forward toward his goal, backward and away from his goal, or to a point where he stalls out in focus. The minute he starts speaking about not feeling well, what seems to follow is a slump in his shoulders, downcast eyes, a caved in posture, followed by less intensity in terms of motivation. When he speaks about something that angers him, his body tenses, he becomes irritable, and his focus is directed away from himself and onto someone else. When the boxer speaks about something that is joyful, he smiles, opens up his posture, and he becomes energized and ready to tackle the training challenges ahead. The fact is that words are not cheap; they are actually quite valuable and extremely telling.

The boxer needs to talk the talk long before he walks the walk. Everything starts with how he thinks, and is followed-up with what he decides to do, and then does. The words we choose, much like that of the boxer, direct us toward emotions that will either energize or debilitate us. As the great Muhammad Ali once said: "What you're thinking is what you're becoming." We need to know what we are saying and how it turns into what we do and how we choose to do it. Unfortunately, most people are not aware of what they say and what it means to their overall performance. We all need to be extremely mindful of the words we choose and what effect they have on us each day. In this chapter we consider the importance of word choices and self-talk in relation to building focus and conviction.

Working on Language

Boxers train in gyms where they become friends with small pockets of teammates. Each pocket is built around a few boxers who are of like mind. When I used to travel with the Canadian National Boxing Team to international tournaments, I would notice that the positive-minded athletes always stuck together. There was also a cohesive pocket of athletes who were uncommitted, and a third pocket that included whiners and under-achievers. Within each pocket, the athletes had a certain sub-culture that was best described in terms of how they spoke, meaning the words they chose to express themselves.

Though few boxers are cognizant of what they say and how it influences their thinking and behaviors, in reality what they say is extremely important. Each time the boxer opens his mouth he influences himself directly, though also indirectly through energy reciprocated by the teammates he surrounds himself with. Those who are at the very pinnacle of the sport are typically constructive thinkers. They focus on what is controllable and then figure out how to impose themselves on their environment, to have a desired effect. Their thinking is confirmed by the words they choose, and when they hear their own words, it synergistically confirms their constructive thinking. These people are not products of their environment – they are often products on their environment.

I spend much of my time working with clients on their word choices. They need to describe themselves, not only in a positive way, but also in a format that engrains a good focus. The words they choose to express themselves are aspects of their self-talk, meaning the language they use, beginning inside their own head. There is also the language they share with the world around them. Every discussion or interview reflects carefully chosen words that in turn send a clear message out into the world. That message has a boomerang effect where what is said then finds its way back to the athlete as media, friends and fans follow the boxer's lead and speak to him using his point of reference.

When you live the parts of your life, from your workplace, to the groups you choose to socialize with, you infuse language into your environment, as do the people around you. What I mean is that you influence your environment and at the same time, you are also influenced by that environment. Think for a moment about the influence you have on those around you. When you stride into your workplace with enthusiasm and energy, people perk up, take notice, open their shoulders, and smile. You in turn are reinforced in your high-energy approach by their response. In those moments, you brought positive energy into your environment, and that energy was bounced back to you as you strode forward to wherever you were going. Now consider a person in your working environment who acts the role of "buzz kill", meaning someone who sucks the oxygen and enthusiasm out of the environment. For the most part, buzz kills are avoided no matter what. If instead you choose to eaves drop on the words they say, most of what leaves their mouth suggests an interpretation that the word is uncontrollable, with the buzz kill as the victim of his environment.

Contenders have no time for people who sap their energy. Each day needs to be tackled as an opportunity to take at least one more step forward toward his overall goal of reaching the summit as a boxer. With a focus on forward movement, he needs to think progressively, and also speak about his proactive decisions. Language confirms a way of thinking, and what we hear becomes what we do. Language is among the most under rated parts of your daily existence in terms of its effect on your thinking and doing. What you say becomes who you are and what you do. Choose your words wisely and you will gain a level of energy and focus each day that will bring you to the next level upward in your life.

Planning the Pre- Battle Message

Many people think that in boxing, the fights are won in the confines of the ring. Two years ago one of my clients spoke to his opponent during a public press conference five days prior to the fight. My client was the challenger and his opponent was the world champion. The champion spoke first, looked at his audience, and promised a great fight. Then it was my client's turn. He stood up, looked at the champion, looked down at himself, and stood silent for just a few seconds.

The champion was wearing jeans and a pullover shirt. My client was wearing a three- piece suit, tie, cufflinks, and perfectly polished, gleaming shoes. The rest of his working team was dressed equally, also in suits. The challenger began, "look at me and then look at my opponent. Tell me who is the champion and who is the challenger". In response, the reigning champion responded that they would see who was who later that week.

The message was carefully crafted in relation to the opponent. The champion was by nature a fighter known to have a volatile temper. When we profiled the champion before starting our training camp we knew in advance that he began boxing to channel his aggression as a result of being a bully. Bullies have short fuses and typically, bullies are the ones who do the bullying. Then again, when bullies are bullied back, they often become silent and submissive. They are not accustomed to being disrespected, nor belittled. The message to the champion was that he would be treated with no respect. The champion was about to be bullied and cut down to size.

Messages are always crafted in relation to your strengths and the Achilles heel of your opponent. The message you and your working team develop should be well informed, based upon carefully gathered research in advance of its delivery. The ultimate goal through the message is to build your conviction and focus while bringing your opponent to a way of thinking that is counter productive to his/her performance. Though most boxers do this sort of strategy intuitively, to deliver a really good message in the form of as knockout punch, you need to know whom that message is intended for, how to reach him, and what the intended outcome should be. Then you go forward and craft the perfect message.

When my client delivered the underlying message to the champion that there would be no respect forthcoming through words and actions, we were not surprised throughout the next few days when the champion started looking submissive; he began to avert eye contact and in front of the press, speak without conviction. What followed a few days later on North American television was the knighting of a new world champion. Though some to this day believe that the fight was won in the ring, our working team began to tenderize the vulnerable - oversized champion several days before the real battle took place.

There is an ideal message for each and every opponent. Your job is to do the research and find out what that message must be. Then all you have to do is deliver it time and again and break down the walls of your opponent's resistance and so, also the space he occupies. In boxing we like to call this strategy "softening up" the opponent. By softening your opponent, you can gain an edge. Don't just go into meetings against an opponent using your intuition on the fly. Though intuition is important, so too are fact-finding missions and targeted messaging.

DOUBLE DIVIDENDS

Our working team is a tightly knit group of people who work closely like a hand and glove. There is no telling where the hand ends and the glove starts. Before every social encounter that our boxers have with an opponent, that boxer sits with us and we work through exactly where we want to go and also where we want to take the opponent. Almost always, our opponent is lured into a trap, before long following us to the exact way of thinking we tempt him toward. Before long the cage slams home and he is left wondering "how in God's name did I get here?". By the time that fighter realizes he is encaged, it is too late to adapt.

Typically, when boxers about to fight come together for some sort of photo opportunity or press / media event, each boxer looks to either bully his adversary. The approach most people take is one-dimensional. Every little encounter holds the possibility of earning the boxer what I like to think of as either a single or double dividend. You know what I mean by a dividend based on your own familiarity with the banking industry. Dividends are what every boxer is looking to gain through his own sound decisions, but few go after the double dividend.

In advance of every encounter between my clients and a forthcoming opponent, I remind the client we are looking for a double dividend. In a stare down when the two boxers face off for the cameras during the press conference, and then a few days later after their weigh-in, our clients always face off with a correctly developed strategy in mind. Sometimes he is the first to face off and he gets right into the personal space of his adversary. Other times, no eye contact is made until the night of the fight. By that time the adversary realizes far too late that my client is more than ready. Still other times we make the adversary wait for a stare down as if to tell him who is going to set the pace and who is going to wait for whom.

The goal, always, is to gain the personal advantage and double that advantage by delivering the best of oneself while simultaneously chipping away at the opponent. Double dividends are typically not achieved in the world of professional boxing, but only because many boxers are unaware, sloppy, or lazy in preparation. The goal is to win the battle before it has ever taken place. Little by little, you are gaining momentum, all the while chipping away at the momentum of your opponent. I agree that few people think in terms of double dividends. Then again, few really reach the summit as performers. Through double dividends, you could level out the playing field and press your own advantage forward.

Working with a Script

Part of talking the talk is knowing when to stick to your script and also, when to improvise. There are touch points that a well-prepared boxer likes to cover off in his consistent messaging to the enemy's camp. These points are anchors that find their way into discussion with the media through radio interviews, television interviews, blogs, press conferences, YouTube broadcasts, social networking pages, and the like.

Some boxers rehearse their speeches and then deliver those speeches word for word. In reality speeches do need some careful scripting. The boxer needs to know where he wants to go and also where he wishes to take his opponent. On the other hand, there needs to be some flexibility within the script so that the boxer can adapt to the audience in front of him and tweak his words so that the intended message is received.

Scripts are meant to be well-informed guidelines, much like a fight strategy requires some flexibility. As the boxer steps into battle there is some modification to the plan, but on the whole, the objective is to stay within one's own plan and in so doing, to take the opponent out of his plan. Every opponent wishes to pull you out of your focus through a script of his own. The boxer able to stick with his script and his strategy will slowly overcome his opposition.

Maybe the success at first won't be visible. Slowly but surely though, if you have the conviction to follow through on your plan, you will forge ahead. The fact is, control starts from within the boxer and then spreads outward to the opponent and the audience. Control can only happen when one anchors strategy within well-developed touch points.

Reminders from Your Corner

- Listen carefully to the words you choose the explain yourself. Words motivate and de-motivate depending on which words are chosen.
- Your strategy for the fight is in part about you and in part about your opponent. Study the opponent well.
- Battles are often won before they are ever fought. Start fighting the battle early, before you ever step into the ring.
- When bantering with the opponent, look to build yourself up and soften your opponent at the same time.
- Talk is important despite what some might think. Talk has value and it sets the stage for what is to come.

STEP FIVE: FIGHT WEEK

There is nothing better than the week of battle when all of your ducks are in a row. Many will tell you that the hard work is now behind you and it is time to perform. There are lots of well known sayings reminding us how wrong people can be when they start "counting their chickens before they are ever hatched".

I have seen athletes gain and lose momentum during fight week. Some think they have things under control and the fight is in the bag. They then decide to coast their way through the week - relaxed. All of a sudden the fight is upon them and these coasting athletes find themselves jolted back to reality. Sometimes, by the time the boxer re-focuses, it is too late. The opponent has taken the fight to him and there is no way to prevent the downhill slide as the opponent backs the boxer up to the ropes, going in for the kill.

The week of battle is all about implementation. The best-organized boxers stick to their plans and actually use this final week to push their positive momentum forward. The pre-bout week then is all about the boxer going inside himself and his team. There is no time for a sideways look, or a diversion into discussions and topics that are off focus and far away from the performance ahead. I have worked with several high profile boxers who've chosen to remain engaged on social network pages and on e-mail, all the while hooked at the hip with their cell phones. Those sorts of athletes were eventually always caught out. There is only so much energy one can invest during fight week and that investment needs to be done with care in relation to the battle ahead.

The week of battle is in my opinion the most important time in a boxer's preparation, providing he has trained with intensity and intelligence to that moment in time. The reason for its importance is that there are lots of places and moments when things can deviate off course and go desperately wrong.

When people have lots of time on their hands, they sometimes tend to twiddle their thumbs and get into all kinds of trouble. The pre-bout week, as you will see, is a time for rest and restoration: it is the calm before the storm.

I have seen first-hand where a poorly managed final week almost cost one particularly gifted world champion his world title. I was working with the athlete and found he was coming and going throughout the day to many social and media events. When fight night came, he started well. As the fight wore on, the opponent proved particularly tough. In the final round, the opponent caught the fatigued champion with an accurate punch and sent him sprawling to the canvas. If it weren't for the ropes, that athlete would have never crawled his way to standing and beat the count. Luckily for that athlete, the final bell went before the opponent could do further damage.

There are always telltale signs when an athlete is not up for the event ahead. The week before the fight is one of those times when the boxer and his team need to look inward, rest, hydrate, eat correctly, do some last minute studying in advance of battle, and take the time to store up energy for the battle ahead. This chapter provides strategies you could use in the week leading up to your championship battle.

Eating Right

There is an old saying that "we are what we eat". Many a boxer has blown an entire career through poor nutrition. There are some boxers who approach their sport with a cavalier attitude, believing that they could eat what they want, drink what they want, and still perform at the upper boundaries of the sport. Eventually these sorts of boxers have their comeuppance and burn out for all of the wrong reasons – primarily built from their neglect.

There is many a boxer who makes it as far as becoming a multi-million dollar athlete, only to burn out as a result of poor eating habits. In the business world outside of professional sport, people again are sloppy in terms of what they choose to eat and drink. They fuel their bodies with either junk food or alternately, a high fat diet. They also drink excessive alcohol and caffeine. Before long, a paunch shows itself and spills over the beltline. The person's face also becomes ruddy, meaning that the kidneys likely are not functioning as well as they should to flush out impurities. Shortly thereafter the person is diagnosed with hypertension, high cholesterol, a sleeping disorder, or excess weight, all suggesting a decline in health.

To be a warrior, you need to feel and look like a warrior. It is critical that you live well, otherwise you just won't have the stamina to engage in daily battle and daily training – your body just won't allow for such demands. Many know their body is failing them and still they do little about it. The decision to eat and drink correctly is an important one that seems to slip through the cracks, at least in Western society. In reality, you cannot ask your body to withstand long-term pressure when you choose to neglect it.

The importance of nutrition compounds within the final week before the fight as the boxer gathers his reserves before his great battle. After all, people cannot step into the ring and expect to do battle if they are missing the most basic of human physiological needs: food and water. In high-level professional boxing, often there is a nutritionist tasked with ensuring that the boxer eats and drinks the correct substances. There is a time for protein, a time for carbohydrates, and a time for fats. The rule of thumb I have come to learn is that the final twenty-four hours should be comprised of pasta and easily digestible proteins such as chicken and fish. The boxer should also try to avoid dairy, as it is mucous producing.

The business-person in final preparation for an important day's meetings should follow the same plan as the professional boxer. The foods she or he eats in advance should be adequate to fuel the body while not creating any stomach upset. There should be lots of hydration through water and not its counterpoint of caffeine. You would be very surprised how often people blow meetings because they are low in blood sugar, have an upset stomach, or have eaten at the wrong time of day in relation to the battle ahead. Eating is a profound part of how the boxer wins his fight, and great battles can only happen when the boxer is fully fueled and armed for battle.

Banking Sleep and Rest

Having a full tank of good nutrition is a great step forward in terms of performance, but eating is only part of the answer to the greatness forthcoming. The warrior also needs a fully charged battery, meaning he/she needs to be bright eyed and bushy tailed. Some would argue they function well on little to no sleep, where others need a full eight hours, or more. Functioning is not what we are looking for when we speak about sleep, meaning what is needed by one's body to fully re-charge. There is a distinct difference between getting by on whatever sleep one can garner and banking the correct amount of sleep and rest.

On average, people need eight hours of sleep a night, most every night. The human body can adapt to less than eight hours sleep and still produce a reasonably good day of performance the following day. However, just as the boxer is not looking to perform at a basic level, he is also not looking for basic physiological needs such as a bare minimum of sleep. Excellence requires a certain level of vigilance and commitment to self-care. The boxer who chooses to be cavalier with his sleep, just as he is sloppy with his diet, eventually short sells himself in terms of career longevity. Fatigue catches up with every boxer sooner or later. Slight fatigue may not show itself in the first few rounds, but it eventually rears its head deeper into the fight when the boxer needs to dig deep.

When we speak about sleep, we are not only speaking about having eight hours banked each night. Though the amount of sleep is very important, so too is the time of night one gains that sleep. There is a significant body of literature about sleep studies where it is affirmed each hour of sleep banked before midnight is worth much more than any hour gained after midnight. People function on a circadian rhythm where they go in and out of deep sleep. The term for this deep sleep is REM sleep, or rapid eye movement sleep. The goal is to bank this deep sleep, which includes dreaming, hopefully when it is dark outside. When the sun comes up in the morning, it is then ideal to wake up, step into the sunlight and absorb Vitamin D.

Finally, there is such a thing as good sleep hygiene. When a boxer returns to his room, the room has to be one that invites rest via low stimulation. The sleep environment needs to be quiet, dimly lit, with no electronic devices, including laptops, wireless devices and video games to stimulate him. Instead, there is something to be said for old-fashioned reading of a paperback, easy listening music, and a bath or shower. There needs to be a prerequisite wind down stage before one eases into a restful sleep – the platform needs to be set for rest in advance of it actually happening. When people wonder why they cannot fall asleep they need to consider whether they have taken the necessary steps to lower their arousal before trying to sleep. Sleep is always the end product of good decisions that end in relaxation and recovery.

Now, the elite boxer has a well-trained body that can withstand all kinds of pressure. To a certain point in his career he can actually get by with minimum amounts of sleep. The high performance entrepreneur, academic, or student can likely also get by with less than optimal amounts of sleep for a little while. If you are one of these people getting by, you need to be kinder with yourself and also, far more careful. Much like the high performance athlete, you need to put every advantage on your side. You need good quality regular sleep in order to be clear minded and focused the following day. The pressure of performance necessitates a much greater amount of self-care than typical daily existence. Sharpness is a relative term, and if you are looking to be razor sharp, sleep is a significant part of your equation.

Sticking within the Team

Fight week is an incredibly exciting time for the contender. After years of sharking his way to the top, he finally has his chance to make his move and dethrone the reigning champion. To be the best, the contender needs to compete against the best, and this week will tell his story.

When the boxer engages in fight week, he does so with his working team. He is not alone, out there by himself. Fight week equates with lots of pressure and expectation based upon his expectations and also the expectations of others, both friends and observers. The contender is preparing to bump up against a worthy adversary, and so pressure is unavoidable.

With pressure, people become edgy, and even the quietest and most easy going of people, sometimes become agitated and hard to get along with. Fight week is when the contender and his team are really tested in terms of their cohesiveness. More times than not, fight week is the undoing for contenders and those they work with. Teams fight in and among themselves and the energy that should be banked and then directed at an opponent is diffused or misdirected inward onto the team. Before long the team falls apart, people stop communicating, and from there, everything goes terribly wrong.

The opposite phenomenon unfolds when pressure synergizes a team to the point where they become closer and even more focused on performance. A tight knit team will eat together, socialize together during activities and bout preparation, communicate that much more openly as the week progresses, and only separate as the members gain their own rest, recharge their batteries, and then prepare to re-engage and contribute energy and focus within their team.

There are always signs when a team is doing what it needs to do in preparation for battle. From the inside people are positive, in sync, and synergistic to the overall functioning of the group. A team wins and loses together. Accountability and pressure is distributed evenly across the team so that all have a stake in the eventual outcome and pressure is also evenly distributed. Fight week will then become the opportunity to test what a team is really made of. When a team is healthy and cohesive pressure only tightens its composition.

If you want to really perform at your best, you cannot make it all the way to the finish line on your own. You need a support team to keep you on the right track. Jesse James, a famous stagecoach robber from the nineteenth century said it best when he told his team "either we hang together or we'll hang alone". Fight week is a time to work together and present a united front, not just to the public eye, but also to the point where those within the team feel that you are all pulling on the same rope, heading in the same well-informed direction.

Dealing with External Demands

To a certain point in a boxer's career, he can manage a wide number of career and personal life demands. As the athlete claws his way closer to the summit however, there is at times a need to narrow in and focus on performance. The challenge is when one becomes a better performer one also becomes more in demand by those in the surrounding environment. The high-end boxer is inundated with interview and media requests, lots of motivational speeches, social functions with sponsors, and requests from a ever-widening group of friends and social affiliations.

It is wonderful to be in demand, and for most performers, this desire to be wanted is both a wish and a curse. Recognition is an important part of the high achiever's advancement to the top. There is a time and place when demands can be met and the elite performer can bask in the sun of recognition. There is also a time and place when external demands take one's focus away from where it needs to – on the performance.

This chapter has been devoted to fight week. For you, fight week might take on an entirely different meaning such as the week of an important interview, an important pitch to a potential consumer, or a pressing exam. Your performance week needs to be geared toward one simple question: "what do I need to do this week in order to achieve excellence in my performance?" The question directly above needs to guide every decision you make during fight week.

Fight week, as I always explain to my clients on the Monday, when the entire week is still in front of us, is entirely about crossroads. Each day we arrive at many crossings where we decide to go left, go right, or proceed straight ahead. The choices we make can either speed up our progression so that we can cross the finish line when we need to, or can slow us in our advancement, sometimes to the point where we sadly cross the line last. Each crossroad is a decision that we make, and the objective especially during fight week, is to identify every crossroad early on and make the decision that takes us in the right direction, toward excellence on fight night.

Most people become bogged down by sloppy, poor decision making. Good decisions are easy to make when questions are encountered one at a time. With crossroads coming at you from every direction, however, sometimes several crossroads are encountered very closely together. Those decisions might be about whether to socialize or rest, when to eat and when to prepare, whether to take an unnecessary phone call, or a pile of other possibilities.

Great decisions are banked with the understanding that your opponents are typically much sloppier in their approach to fight week. If you want a great performance, you need to make great decisions consistently along the way. Fight week is about a progressively narrowing in focus. That focus needs to be placed exclusively and entirely on preparation, nutrition and hydration, rest, and team coordination. The formula for success is easy to follow in principle.

On the other hand, those on the fringes often won't really understand why you are making the tough decisions that need to be made during fight week. Most people don't make the right decisions in advance of their own battles, so you cannot expect them to support you in your correct and disciplined decisions. Just the same, you have to stick to your guns, and turn down invites that take you away from your focus. In professional boxing there is one interviewer who asks misinformed questions that bother boxers. He has interviewed several of my clients many times. Far away from a fight, irritating questions are not that critical in terms of the boxer's mindset. However, I make certain that interviewer does not gain access to my clients in the final few days pre-bout. The reason why is that the media person doesn't even understand how negative his approach is with the elite athletes he interviews. For the outsider such as the above media person, ignorance is bliss. For the boxer, when those sorts of people are encountered, they become a crossroad.

You are not alone in setting the decisions for fight week. You also have a working team that needs to support these decisions – to help keep you on track. You can likely make many good decisions during fight week, and each decision will move you closer to impending success. Your working team is there to help you pick up the final few crumbs and support you in decisions you might have otherwise overlooked or incorrectly responded to. They should also act as your bodyguards, so to speak. They need to not only help you set boundaries with others, but also act on your behalf. Let the team do their job and buffer you from unnecessary distractions that would otherwise take away from your valuable focus and positive momentum.

BRIEFINGS

Focus is not only gained by making good decisions; it is also built through briefings. Briefings are the sorts of meetings that should happen at the beginning and end of each day to ensure you and your team are all pulling on the same rope, in the same direction during each of the final few days pre-bout. The focus for morning briefings is to set the structure for the day ahead and also to ensure that each member is on the same page. Concurrently, there is emotional strength in numbers, with the numbers that count being the core members of your team.

The end of day briefing is set last thing before you and your working team return to your rooms for a good night's sleep. During the end of day briefing the team goes around the circle and provides feedback about the day's events. Some of that feedback should be about things that might have slipped through the cracks. There is no such thing as the perfect day, where everything is perfectly executed. So, debriefing about minor mistakes and oversights helps sharpen and narrow your team's focus, building toward an even better day of bout preparation the following day. The meeting then ends with an acknowledgement of the things that went right so they can be repeated as part of the approach to tomorrow.

Underpinning the two meetings each day is the importance of communication. Under pressure, most people choose not to communicate, and when things concern them, they keep those concerns to themselves. Then, after a poor performance, people slowly come forward and admit that they knew they and their team were off course, but didn't want to voice their concerns during that crucial last week. The goal during fight week meetings is to put everything on the table, for better and for worse. When things are on the table, the team maintains a solid understanding of one another and the team as a whole. From understanding comes confidence, from confidence comes conviction, and from conviction comes great performance and a great result.

Now, I know that you may not have a team of people working with you if you are in an individual enterprise. However, in workplace environments, you need to build a team around you. If you are a student, again, you need to study with at least one classmate who can push you and challenge you, with you doing the same for him or her. If you are working solo, still take the time each morning and evening to debrief yourself. Use the morning to set your plan for the day. In the evening work through an even-handed approach where you look at how you devoted your time for better and worse. Then learn what you need to learn and move forward after a good night's rest to the next day of pre-bout preparation. Fight week is built around small bites of time and even if you find you are wandering off course, you often have the time to correct your navigation. The goal is to use that time wisely and when needed, you must also respond.

Reminders from Your Corner

- Nutrition and hydration are profound parts of excellence. You are what you eat, and also what you drink. Eat well and stay hydrated.
- You need to bank sleep, rest, and all other good decisions religiously. When people become sloppy in their self-care they don't see the consequences until it is too late and the fight is upon them.
- Stay within your team during fight week. You need to engage in "tunneling", meaning that you and your team need to hang together, especially as pressure mounts.
- Devote fight week only to demands that take you closer to perform. Cut out all of the irrelevant demands that will zap your energy and focus.
- Debrief at the beginning and of each day.

STEP SIX: THE WEIGH-IN

There is an old saying that "you need to look your opponent in the eye". Weighing-in before the bout happens about twenty-four hours prior to the fight. The two contenders each make weight, meaning they are evaluated as making the grade in terms of their physical qualifications in advance of the bout. Once both boxers make their requisite weight, they are asked to stand toe to toe and engage in a stare down. The first person who blinks loses the advantage to the person who holds steady eye contact. Many a win and a loss happen at the weigh-in.

Boxers smell fear a mile away. It is visible to the eye, to the ears, and even at the visceral level. Fearful opponents look away, shrink in their posture, quiet in their tone, and they even tremble or shuffle from side to side during the stare down. The thing about boxing is the more assertive – aggressive boxer will often starve his opponent of oxygen and opportunity to expand in size by towering over him. The best boxers know this little detail and some deliberately snip away at their opponents until those opponents are nothing other than a trembling shell. One boxer must be big dog; the other little dog.

Every performer comes face to face with an opponent they need to stare down on. It might be a person you go nose to nose against, it might be a tough task that challenges your self-confidence. Whatever it is, you need to stare back at it and push your conviction forward. You can only do battle with the challenge ahead if, beforehand, you look it square in the eyes and chop it down to its right size. You are the big dog, and the task or opponent in front of you needs to be regarded in its right size.

A few years ago I traveled to England with a client about to fight for his first world title. His adversary was undefeated with a high knockout statistic, meaning the adversary was dangerous. When the two boxers squared off and looked eye to eye the day before battle, the Englishman looked into the eyes of my client and saw something that troubled him – an athlete who looked straight back at him. As the Englishman nattered away in my client's ear trying to discourage him, my client looked back and said: "stop looking into my ear. Look me in the eyes". At the very instance the Englishman was silent for the first time in his career. I could only imagine what the next twenty-four hours might have felt like for the opponent. The opponent was in his own hometown and my client was from across the ocean. How could it be that the person traveling was so self-assured?

Contenders need to be ready, not only to fight, but in advance, to look their challenge back squarely, right in the eyes. When promising boxers shy away from this step of looking their opponent in the eyes, the opponent gains the upper hand, and often keeps it from that builds upon it onward to the end of the fight. As the best of contenders take steps forward in their career, they need to increase their size of posture. Sadly, most boxers shrink as their important bouts approach and in the final few days before performance, sweat themselves down to a smaller size than they should be through needless worry.

Your challenge might or might not be a person as the opponent I just described. Just the same you need to look that challenge in the eye, especially as the date to face the challenge is fast approaching. It is one thing to say you are going to face a challenge several months in advance, and an entirely other thing to actually look that challenge in the eye just before you face it, and still mean what you say. Far too often, people back out of challenges in those final few hours instead of standing toe to toe with the challenge with a daring look. People really find out what they are made of in the face of adversity – just before they encounter it. On the other hand, if you never stand up and face a challenge, you will never find out the scope of your abilities – you will never advance beyond promise, onward to reality.

SWAGGER

Being a contender is all about walking the walk. There is a certain look and demeanor to the champion in the making. That look is in part about a strut, or a swagger. Should you visit videos posted on the web you will find the boxers who weigh-in on the day before they become world champions are virtually shining. They shine to a gleam, and they have a twinkle in their eyes. The twinkle is an all-knowing look that reflects certainty on their part, whilst provoking fear and uncertainty at the gut level from their opponents and their working teams.

The swagger is visible to the eye, starting with the way the contender holds and carries his body. I work with my clients on the way they are to walk their way into the building en route to the scales. The body is open and assertive. The walk is confident, forward moving, smooth, and without falter. The head is held high with eyes straight ahead. On the whole, when the contender with swagger enters the room, he is full size and almost larger than life. The job of the contender is to grow in size and assert his dominance, even in advance of the encounter to come.

When the contender opens up his posture and adopts a visible swagger, the benefit comes in the form of a double dividend. One benefit is direct, through the confidence instilled within him, just by opening his posture. When people open their postures, they automatically feel more confidence and conviction. People only open their postures when they are ready to be seen as full sized and as the big dog. Therefore, by opening the posture, the contender ensures he is on the right track and readying to assert himself in the face of battle. He is ready for fight, not flight.

The second advantage, or second dividend happens indirectly through the eyes of the opponent. When the opponent sees the contender in front of him as growing in size, and looking huge, the opponent realizes that he has a serious fight on his hands. The fight is not going to be easy as he once thought. Boxing is all about one person growing larger and the other growing smaller through tactics outside and then within the confines of the ring. As I said earlier when quoting Sun Tzu: the fight is often won before it is ever fought.

Outside of boxing, there is a lot to learn from the contender's swagger. First, to be upwardly mobile you need to look like a person on the move. You need to carry yourself in a way where you will be noticed. Some people fail to carry themselves, and as a result, despite their qualifications, they are overlooked due to a lack of charisma. Others are selected for plumb positions because they have the walk that promises they will be noticed time and again. People in leadership positions need to be noticed through an open posture, an assertive gait, and solid eye contact. The bottom line is that if you feel full sized and you look full sized, you have the best chance of reaching your potential; your complete self.

Taking Center Stage

The next step in a pre-bout strategy is to return to center stage after staring down the opponent. Far too often people retreat to the comfort of their home and their personal shell to re-energize and replenish self-confidence. Though it is counter intuitive, when opponents exit center stage, the best of contenders stay there and bask in the sunlight for a little longer. Center stage is something the contender takes possession of and only relinquishes when he has to, and not before.

The challenge that each of us face is to push ourselves forward in the face of adversity, and doing so consistently until we get what we want. Most people push a little, step back a little, and then push again. The approach makes for an inconsistent experience where we often aren't able to see our convictions through to their end. Assertiveness and conviction is not a part-time story. If you want something you need to go after it with thirst, aggression, and consistency. You need to take center stage, and then keep center stage no matter what. Though a working team has your back, you need to stand exposed to the elements, in front of the challenge, with your actions suggesting that you are here to stay.

Center stage is not for the faint of heart. As you stand there, you open yourself to the observations and evaluations of those around you. People will take notice and some will have a difficult time with your assertive approach and dominant demeanor. People without the confidence to take center stage will inside look at you and think how is it that this person has so much confidence and conviction? Outwardly, these same people will possibly criticize you. If you have experienced the harsh judgments of people who dare not in their own right take center stage, you know what I am talking about. By stepping forward and staying at center stage, regardless of what others think, you will take one more importance step forward to asserting yourself onto your opponent or challenge.

Strategic Disengagement

Messages in advance of battle need to have a very big bang for the dollar. The message and strategies the boxer is looking to make should always have maximum impact. When there is a short amount of time in between the pre-battle message and the battle itself, the objective is to leave a resonating idea in the opponent's mind. What the opponent remembers most when there is a short time between the message and the battle are your last words and actions. In social psychology they like to term this phenomenon a "recency effect". The bottom line is the final messages to the opponent are extremely important.

If delivered effectively, they can soften up the opponent and gain you more of an edge than many people appreciate.

There is a time to engage before a fight and also a time to disengage. The wise boxer knows and understands when it is time for each part of his pre-bout weigh-in experience, and then follows his plan to the letter. It's not easy to execute what the boxer agrees to in principle, and yet the best prepared and managed boxers keep to their strategies, making themselves visible only when it stands to benefit them and disadvantage their opponents.

Strategic disengagement is not just about when the boxer arrives and departs from a pre-bout encounter. It also includes how the boxer engages with those around him.

Many spectators and media like to press palms with the contender. People like to be part of greatness, they like to see it and also touch it. Each time the contender offers his hand, he is also offering up good will and friendship, among others types of energy investment.

Disengagement is a necessary piece to the fighter's strategy, and that disengagement includes no longer "pressing the flesh" with people in the environment. Instead, the new action of touching fists keeps the boxer's energy and focus within him.

Many years ago, I travelled with a boxer to Germany. The boxer is an amazing person and he was a fantastic world champion. We went to Germany so that he could defend his world title in the home city of his highly respected opponent. After the weigh-in my client hung around and shook hands with many of the people there for the spectacle. He and his team were enjoying the moment – we were basking in our glory. Little did we know that on the very next evening my client would be the champion no more. He did perform well that night and to this day, many believe he should have retained his title. However, looking back in retrospect we were all very comfortable going into the fight – too much so. In hanging around the weigh-in for too long afterward, he and his team did give away much of our advantage and our energy.

People in all realms of performance sometimes outstay their welcome in their performance environments. There is a time to make yourself visible and a time to make yourself invisible.

The goal is to leave a message and then allow that message to grow in the imagination of the opponent. In relation to a looming battle, the goal is for the opponent's imagination to run wild as she/he recalls your physical presence, delivered through a very well choreographed encounter. The bottom line is you need to know when it is time to deliver a message and also when it is time to disappear, with the message left to do its work.

REPLENISHING RESOURCES BEFORE THE BATTLE

There is a certain point before the battle when all of the work has been done. The athlete has prepared every little detail in advance of the contest, and there is nothing else to do. The wisest and best managed of athletes know when they reach this point of readiness in their preparation. When the athlete has achieved complete readiness, with nothing left to do, the goal is to replenish all of his resources and make certain that he eats well, is perfectly hydrated, adequately rested, and perfectly calm.

At the opposite end of the continuum, some boxers squander away their readiness by spinning their wheels in the final twenty-four hours before battle. They try to squeeze in meetings, sessions, e-mails, and the sorts of exchanges that pull their focus outside of their own bodies. These people eventually waste their energy and show up for fight night emotionally flat and extremely vulnerable.

It is not unheard of for the best-prepared boxer to lose his fight within the final few hours before performance. The simplest self-care strategies of eating, hydrating and resting are pushed off to the side and instead, the boxers engage in "busy work", filling their day with irrelevant activities they won't recall shortly afterward. To battle with the best of opponents, the fighter needs huge stores of energy and focus. Guidance from the working team can take the boxer part of the way to complete energy storage in advance of the bout. The boxer needs to go the rest of the way in terms of self-care on his own.

When I was an under-graduate university student, I recall sitting in the corridors of many an exam hall. Some students looked relaxed, inwardly focused, and ready for the task at hand. Others were still cramming information and trying to memorize details, even as they were walking into the exam hall. I have tried both strategies, and quieting the mind and body before battle always works best.

There comes a point in time where you need to go with what you've got and what you know. I like to think of this moment as a "leap of faith". Every performer needs to take a leap of faith and trust that his work is done. For some people it is a struggle to stop working and take a breath in the final hours before battle. However, in reality there comes a point where you can no longer pick up any more crumbs of information and detail The best executed of performances come from a clear and relaxed mind; one that is sharp, energized and ready for battle. Excellence comes from clarity and clarity comes from being at peace with who you are, what you know, and the fact that you prepared well for the battle to come.

Reminders from Your Corner

- Champions in the making have a certain swag. Swagger is built from an open posture, an energetic walk stride, and vibrating energy. Enter every achievement setting with physical presence.
- When you square off against an opponent, look that person in the eye and never sever contact. You need to be dominant and larger than life.
- Always be ready to take center stage and overshadow your opponent. Physical presence is an important part of winning the battle before it is ever fought.
- Know when it is time to show your face in advance of battle and also when it is time to disengage. The goal is to sensitize your opponent to your message, not desensitize.
- The last twenty-four hours before the performance, your focus must shift to basic self-care and away from any further physical or mental preparation.

Step Seven: The Final Twenty-Four Hours

Everything the contender has ever worked for is about to reveal itself before the final few hours come to an end. Some boxers spend these last hours going inside themselves where others try to do most any activity to stay busy and distracted from the pending performance. There is no avoiding the last minute jitters that every great performer experiences as the final few hours wind down on the clock. Some experience butterflies, others fears and self-questioning. In reality even the best of world-class boxers experience a full case of the jitters late in the game. So, it's not so much a matter of whether the athlete experiences the butterflies or not, but rather about having those butterflies fly in formation. Nervousness is a symptom that the boxer is alive and ticking. The energy revealed through nervousness suggests that he is alert and ready to go to battle.

With no real hurdles to clear any longer other than the battle itself, the contender needs to now focus on stoking his energy so that when the time comes, he is able to channel it into his performance and onto his opponent. The self-focus needed in the final few hours makes or breaks many a boxer as he goes through his last few crossroads. One crossroad is to dine before the last night's sleep with the working team or to sit with a wider group of friends and attend to the expansive conversation. Obviously, there is little energy to spare and so dining with friends, though typically lots of fun, is not the best decision. Another crossroad might be whether to wind down for the evening early and spend the final few hours before sleep in a relaxing activity such as reading and listening to music, or to surf the net.

Many a prospect never stops to reflect and then realize how valuable each crossroad is during the final few hours pre-bout, in terms of his future. One well-chosen crossroad followed by another, and then a third, will amount to quite an investment in the contender's future. The fact is crossroads should not be squandered and good decisions in the final few hours are synergistic with each one contributing momentum toward final readiness for battle. In this chapter we will consider some of the physical and psychological strategies that will build your focus in the final twenty-four hours before you engage in battle.

Dining with the Team the Day before Battle

The pre-performance day meals are important moments for the performer. Nutrition and hydration are two basic needs that the body requires to function at his best. Even when meals incorporate the correct nutrients and components, they can either enhance or take away from performance. The reason why is because the contender has to be in the correct frame of mind to really gain from his meal. I am certain you have eaten in company at one point and also in isolation at another point in time. When people eat alone, they often rush through their meals, all the while feeling alone and even isolated. Mealtimes, especially so close to the moment of performance, need to include the correct components. These components extend beyond nutrition and onward to the company that is kept. That company needs to be supportive, though also, there must be a balance struck between how many supporters are too few and too many.

Not long ago I was part of a team dinner with a world champion eating his pre-performance meal, just before fighting to defend his world title. We all sat together, as we did during several fights before that point. However, for that particular meal, something was very different. The champion was restless and his eyes darted around the table as he worried about what others were thinking. Now typically, the champ ate only with his working team and less than a handful of his closest friends. This time, however, he decided on his own to include his girlfriend, her siblings and parents. Instead of sitting and eating his meal in a relaxed state, the boxer stood up part way through his meal and sat beside his girlfriend, making small talk with her and her family. I have known the champion for quite some time and what I noticed was that he was expending a lot of energy; energy he would soon need for the fight of his life.

Many years before, I worked with a world champion from Eastern Europe. He has long since retired. I recall sitting with that athlete the night before his battle day at a huge evening meal. The athlete's entire team surrounded him, including me, his coaching staff, managers, friends, and family. As we began to eat I noticed that the boxer was nervous and also frustrated. The sheer volume of people upset the athlete and almost immediately, he stood and stepped away from the table. He, one of his closest friends and I went for a walk. He was about to fight against another world champion in the fight of his life. He didn't have the interest in sitting and making small talk during that crucial juncture in his professional life. Looking back on that moment, the boxer was not being difficult. He was simply protecting his energy and focus. He needed to look inside himself before battle, and doing so was impossible in a large social setting.

The pre-performance meal is all about stoking the fire found within the fighter's body, mind and soul. There are only so many things the fighter can focus on as he nourishes himself and narrows his focus. Though meals are often a social event where it is good manners to eat, chat, and hang out with friends and loved ones, not in the case of the pre-fight meal. Pre-bout meals are entirely and exclusively about the fighter charging his battery for the fight ahead through fuel and the conservation of energy. The people chosen to dine with the fighter during this crucial pre-performance time must be energizing and also supportive of the athlete going inside himself.

When you dine the evening before battle day, you can choose to dine alone or with company. Should you choose to eat with company, the people you choose need to understand just how important the fight ahead is for you. These people are there to support you in their attendance, and not to draw your energy through needless conversation. Remember, there are times when conversation bolsters energy, and times where it can deplete the performer. Select your dining company wisely when fueling for battle. You only have so much energy to spend and you need to protect that energy much like a dog protects its bone.

Sleeping or Sleeplessness

It seems that performers, be they athletes or otherwise, sometimes struggle to sleep. Highly popular magazines feature advertisements for all kinds of sedatives. Most high performance boxers do not require daily assistance with their sleep, likely because they lead such physically active lifestyles. However, the night before the day of battle presents its challenges when it comes to banking that final night's sleep. Even the best of sleepers can experience a sleepless night just before they engage in battle.

When I first started consulting in elite boxing, I was the motivational coach with the Canadian National Boxing Team. On the very first day of my work, I met a talented boxer known to under achieve during important international tournaments. The very first question he asked me was how to wind down and sleep the night before critical fights. The question he asked received quite a few head nods from his teammates. It seemed that even the best of amateur elite boxers struggled with their sleep the night before the day of battle.

For every competitor, there are patterns in how she/he goes about preparing for important battles. These patterns likely surface before the competitor ever becomes an elite athlete. One or a few consecutive sleepless nights just before the day of competition leave the competitor with the belief that he just won't sleep the night before battle. With that belief in mind, the performer then approaches the competitions that follow with the belief that no sleep will occur during that final night before the battle.

People engage in patterns of belief that often trace back to one or a few random and isolated incidents. There is an entire - comprehensive body of literature found in the area of positive psychology, termed resilience. People tend to give up on their resilience and good habits, and instead buy into a belief system that takes them away from the opportunity to perform at their best. People hamstring themselves with incorrect - negative thinking, supported by incorrect strategies.

Sleeping is an important part of what the performer needs, ideally, before the day of battle. To sleep, the performer needs to take the opportunity and wind down in advance of any sleep attempt. The sorts of activities I always promote to my clients have included reading, listening to soft music, going for a walk, taking a warm bath or shower, meditation, and relaxation yoga. What all of these activities have in common is that they lower the performer's nervousness by lowering and deepening breathing and relaxing the body, mind and spirit. Relaxing activities then become the springboard upon which to enter into an even more relaxing activity: sleep. Without relaxation in advance of sleep, there is less chance that you will be able to let gain rest.

Some athletes also believe that if they don't sleep the night before they perform, that all is lost. Let me tell you, that belief is off base, meaning incorrect. There will be the isolated time where you will make incorrect pre-sleep decisions that will take away from your night's sleep. You might land up reading your e-mail that one last time, only to find an irritating or upsetting message. There will also be evenings that will have followed an argument with a loved one, important colleague or friend. When people have frustrating days, or engage in irritable thinking just before they attempt to bank sleep, chances are they have sold themselves short in in their resting that night. There are also evenings when people just cannot get to sleep no matter what.

Many an athlete has experienced a sleepless night before competing in an Olympic final, a world championship fight or some other performance of extreme importance. The first step to minimizing the risks and downside of a sleepless night is to accept that you are not sleeping. One night of sleeplessness does not make for an exhausted performer, assuming you realize this as a fact. There also might be times the following day when you can regain sleep, should your body tell you that you need it. People perform under all kinds of stress and hardship, and I have witnessed numerous boxers win their bout in spite of a sleepless night. One such boxer mentioned previously, did not sleep one wink the night before he became a world champion.

Filling the Day

The day of battle is finally upon the contender. It is time to channel that energy and engage in the final preparation strategies for fight night. What the boxer chooses to do with his time in the final few hours either confirms him as on the right track or sadly, undoes many hard months of preparation. Though many boxers don't fully understand it, the final few hours can make or break the boxer. The goal is to make those final few hours and the associated decisions count in a positive way.

The day begins with a good meal. A good meal, as you already know, is partly about what you eat and partly about whom you eat with. What you eat has to fuel your energy stores. My fighters and I are all advocates for clean food, especially just before the boxer goes into battle. What the boxer puts into his stomach needs to break down easily and also build his energy stores. Clean foods might include organics, a curtail on dairy, clear non-alcohol fluids, cereals, and fish or chicken – broiled, not fried.

Who the boxer sits with must also align with his approach to nutrition. The person(s) he is sitting with, and it should only be one or two people, should be tidy, focused people. These dining guests of the contender need to be positive, constructive, and easy on his digestive system. He needs to digest what they say as he goes through and reviews the next few hours ahead and how to use it these hours to build momentum and energy.

Next, there must also be time for the fighter to go inside of himself, without distraction. This step forward in the day should usually follow the meal. The contender knows what he needs to do based on the morning briefing; now he has to connect the dots and move forward in his progress. Some fighters struggle with being left alone, but then again, the fighter will eventually be alone in the ring when he faces off against his opponent. The clarity he will need in the fight has to be established before the fight, in the final hours; that clarity cannot be established when he is attending to other people. It is a time for solitude.

Throughout the day, however, it is also good for the fighter to touch base with his working team and go for a walk. Touching base ensures from the vantage of his working team that the fighter is tracking along correctly toward the performance ahead. Sometimes a working team member will spot something in the fighter that isn't quite right. So, a walk will allow the working team member to engage in a sort of quality assurance ride along. The fighter is the best versed people when it comes to how he feels, but just the same, sometimes things can be spotted from the outside, looking in. For example, one might spot the fighter breathing from his chest, and not breathing deeply. By pointing out this little observation to the fighter, he will become more self-aware, take in more oxygen, and return to clearer thinking.

The way you go about your day in advance of the challenge will also make or break you! You need to set the stage for a great performance by eating well, allowing yourself time to build energy, and also by ensuring that someone you know and trust can eyeball you and double check that you look right. Between what you know and feel and also the judgment of someone you trust, you will have covered off all of the bases in terms of your final preparation. The last few hours before battle are important ones to you: make them count.

PACKING

Packing is much more than a mechanical procedure; to the competitor it is a monumental step forward in terms of final battle readiness. More professional boxers than not depart from the hotel on the way to the boxing arena, all the while wondering whether they packed everything they needed for the battle ahead. When I used to consult with Canada's Olympic Boxing Team, I also provided an extensive reminder to the athletes to pack with care each day before they departed for the Olympic venue. Despite all of my warnings and suggested strategies, there would be at least two boxers at every international competition who lost monumental battles as a result of how they arrived at the arena. The diversion away from success would happen just after they realized they forgot an essential piece of equipment such as their shorts, shirts, or mouth guard.

The organized contender is a person who packs with the utmost of care, a few hours before he departs to the competition arena. He takes every item out of his equipment bag, places all of his equipment on his bed, and then proceeds to re-pack the items one by one. As he places the pieces of equipment in his bag, he checks the item off on his packing list with a red pen. By the time the equipment bag is carefully packed, there is absolutely no question in his mind that everything needed for battle is there at his fingertips.

In stark contrast, many a contender has blown his contender status as a result of disorganization. Performances are done and also undone as a result of "question marks" just before battle. The boxer who is readying to perform at his best commits to removing as many of the question marks that he can before the battle. He believes that the fewer questions marks remain, the better it is in terms of his bottom line performance. Consider this: have you ever gone off to an important meeting or interview and wondered as you were traveling to that meeting whether you have forgotten something you might need to perform?

The best performances are built from preparation in terms of content, but also through an organized approach. The business-person needs pens, paper, appropriate clothing, a well-organized computer, back-ups of documents and slideshows saved within the computer, and whatever else is needed to pull off that great performance. There is really no need to arrive at the big presentation without your computer or slideshow saved correctly. There is no reason to leave things to chance as a result of sloppy packing. You need to be extremely organized and methodical in order to transition from contender to champion.

On Time Is Late

Many years ago, while I was gaining my doctoral education, I engaged in a research project and interviewed some of the world's best internationally renowned sport administrators. They included executive members of the International Olympic Committee and the International Paralympic Committee, among a few other high profile sport managers. I sat with each of these people and asked her or him what made that person tick in their professional life. To that point in my own existence I was habitually on time or slightly late for most every scheduled appointment. One of the interviews, however, changed my perspective regarding being organized. I remember the

President of the International Paralympic Association sharing a saying with me: “if you are on time, you’re late”.

Earlier this year one of my clients was in for the fight of his life against one of the best pound for pound boxers in the world. My client has a tremendous working team; we are all organized people who try to minimize losses in performance by adhering to schedules. The boxer on the other hand is habitually late for everything, be it air travel, appointments with the media, or workout sessions. The boxer has managed to reach the very pinnacle of boxing despite being extremely careless and reckless in his scheduling. Though lateness doesn’t seem to faze the boxer, it definitely affects his working team and so, indirectly the boxer is compromised. People don’t perform in a vacuum.

When preparing contenders for the battles of their life much of the organization and structure is developed to deliver them to their fight in the best possible physical and mental shape.

The mental aspect of the preparation is in part developed well in advance of battle. However, one of the resonating messages I have shared in this chapter has been that lots of hard work can be undone in a very short period of time, just before battle. So, the goal is to schedule the week and the day of battle very carefully so that the contender and his working team know exactly where they need to be, when they need to be there, and why. Nothing is left to chance, and we allow for inevitable setbacks, including flat tires, car breakdowns, traffic, and every other possible road bump that will compromise the opponent and his working team, but not us.

If you have an important interview, meeting, or presentation, you need to be there in advance of the scheduled time. Technology needs to work perfectly and you also need time to gather yourself for the battle ahead. Though some people will arrive at the scheduled time and manage to pull of their victory, those people also leave a lot to chance. Life is if nothing else, unpredictable. Schedules change and time setbacks often happen. When you organize your day and arrive ahead of schedule, you will sooner or later avert a setback by being early for each and every appointment.

Reminders from Your Corner

- During the last twenty-four hours before battle you need to go into the performance bubble and affiliate only with your team. Though social friends are an important part of every performer’s life, there is a place and a time for socializing. The last twenty-four hours before battle is not that time.

- Sleeping and rest are important components you need for battle. Just as you need to bank your sleep the week of the fight, the night before the fight you should follow a program that permits you to wind down and enter into a deep sleep. If by chance you have a sleepless night, no worries. Even the best of world-class performers can pull off victory after one sleepless night.
- Structure the day of battle so that you are able to slowly narrow your attention onto the battle ahead. Throughout the day touch base with a central member of your working team to double check that you are on track.
- Know what you need in advance of the battle and make certain that you have all of the necessary items. Then take the next step and pack your own equipment carefully, always checking off items from your packing list as they are being packed.
- If you are on time, you're late. Be early enough for every appointment so that you can organize your materials and ensure that whatever technology you need is in working order.

STEP EIGHT: PERFORMANCE WARMING

The moment has arrived and the contender has just pulled in to the competition arena. The cameras pan to the contender's face. What the audience should witness is an extremely focused boxer prepared and ready to battle with his life – someone ready to put everything on the line.

The boxer walks with a mission toward his dressing room. He looks at the camera with solid eye contact and his physical presence is larger than life. The contender's posture is fully open and he is energized in his walk. If there were a wall in front of the contender, it seems he would walk right through it to get to where he needs to go: his warm-up room.

The time needed for a correct warm-up cannot be rushed, but should not divert the time and energy that needs to be invested in the battle ahead. The amount of time and energy needed for the warming process has to be perfect. There is no margin for error when the contender is arming to produce the performance of his life.

The warming process ahead is meant to bring the contender to life, so that his body and mind are fluid and agile. His reflexes must be perfect, he has to think on his feet, use all of the fancy footwork developed in training, and then when the time comes, strike with force, fluidity, and conviction. To get to this point of execution in the ring, the boxer needs to ensure all of his systems (body, mind, spirit) are warmed, much like a pilot needs to run through a checklist before leaving the gate, taxiing to the runway, and then taking flight. The warming process brings the contender to the right frame of reference, needed to take the battle out of his opponent.

The warming process is something that great performers engage in, the world over. Before I deliver an important address to an academic or professional crowd, I need to warm into the ideas I am about to share in my speech. I need to be ready, but not overly tense. My tendency is to pace the room and move around before the scheduled speech – like a caged tiger ready to pounce. You, the boxer and I are not all that different. To be a contender, you need to warm into the state of mind needed to deliver your message: your performance. You cannot just get up and deliver your ideas without being fully warmed, focused and ready for battle.

When people try to perform without a warming process, they are eventually caught off guard by a question or a challenge that will take them off course - away from their battle plan. You need to be awake, warmed and ready to battle at your fullest. This chapter is all about how to sharpen your senses for victory.

Owning the Environment

When boxers are at the top of their game, they seem to own most every environment they step in to. There is no time and place "owning" is more important than during the moment the boxer steps on site at the performance arena.

A feeling of ownership over one's territory is something most every dominant person must feel before he does battle. For the boxer, that territory needs to extend to the entire building, from the entranceway, through the corridors, into the dressing room, and then onward to the ring.

The contender enters his warming area and is met by his working and a few sponsors or supporters. As he walks into the room he claims the space as his own, takes as much of the room as he needs, and then physically begins to occupy the space. He sets down his equipment needed for a thorough and complete warming process. From the manner through which the contender takes possession of the room, people around him figure out very quickly how to work in tandem. The contender is warming to do battle and he needs the space to warm into his fighting self.

When you walk into the building where you will be doing battle you are actually starting your warming process. You need to be the person at the center of the performance.

You need to own the building in order to own those presently occupying the various spaces within it. People tend to stand back when they see someone in charge – the dominant person who owns the physical space. You need to see the performance arena as yours alone. When you approach the battle arena as the big dog, more often than not, others will begin to work around you, listen carefully to what you have to say, and the illusion of control becomes reality.

STRETCHING THE BODY

Contenders understand that to be warmed for performance they need a limber body. The sharpest mind without a limber body will disconnect thinking and the capacity to follow through on that thinking. The objective is to end the warming process with the performer's body is fast, sharp, accurate, and agile. All of the contender's physical skills have to be at his fingertips so that he could call on his body and instantaneously, it will be there ready to pounce.

The opposite of readiness happens to many of the most promising high-end boxers. Some boxers are called "slow starters". These boxers and those who train them actually believe the boxers are and will always be slow in their physical reflexes at the beginning of battle. What these people don't fully understand is that by starting slow, they are automatically placing themselves behind the eight ball, where they have to eventually surge and gain the advantage, coming from behind.

There is no such thing as an innately physical slow starter. However, there is such as thing as an under-warmed performer. People need to be limber and agile to perform at their capacity. The body must be free of any rust and stiffness. Indeed, the best of boxers understand this process well and win their fights from the beginning, by gaining a progressive advantage over their opponent. Wins are often accumulated a little bit at a time, inch by inch.

When a performer makes her or his pitch to a group of people, it is important for that person to have all of the necessary advantages. Part of what makes an idea tantalizing is how the salesperson presents it. If the person is charismatic, fluid, agile, loose in body and open in posture, that person is able to effectively sell the concept or idea. Consider motivational speakers like Anthony Robbins. Great performers such as Robbins hone their sales strategies to a fine art. Selling yourself is something you will be doing for all of your life, no matter your profession – and selling is a performance. You need to look the part and act the part of performer in order to eventually be the part from the inside looking out and from the outside looking in.

So, what should your warming process include? You need an ample amount of time each morning to stretch your body, from your neck down to your toes and your heels. Your body is what is going to transport you into battle and onward to victory. When stretching, you need to also breath deeply, breathing in through your nose and out through your mouth. When you watch the best of professional boxers warming up before a match on global television, notice that every one of them goes through detailed stretching.

Next, within the final twenty minutes before you engage in battle you need to elevate your heart rate. You need to get the blood flowing, though only to the level needed for battle, and no more. You can do so by bouncing up and down, rolling your neck, moving your arms in large circles, and then taking one last stretch of your larger muscle groups (e.g., arms, legs, back). With your body sharpened, you will enliven your senses. Before long your mind will follow suit and you will find that your attention is narrowed and focused on your target.

Freeing the Mind

What differentiates a great performance from an average one is the contender's ability to free his mind. Far too often, contenders become trapped in their own thinking and fail to notice what is going on in the performance. When sports commentators witness boxers with a trapped mind they speak about how that person needs to "let his hands go". What the commentators suggest is actually correct and with merit. There comes a point in time where you have to trust yourself and let go.

At the opposite end of the spectrum, the contender on his way to becoming a champion warms into his performance, so that by the end of his warm-up, he is very much in the moment, ready to embrace the opportunities to come in battle.

It's easy to spot a boxer who is in the moment. He is focused on the task at hand, walks to the ring, never noticing the audience or the irrelevant distractions that exist in every performer's environment. He is on a mission, his vision is narrow and he is committed to keeping that approach from the end of his warm-up through to the final bell and the win.

People often times forget to acknowledge all of the good work they've done in preparation for their performance, and in doing so, minimize their advantage. Students who've done a complete job studying for an exam sometimes panic and fail to acknowledge the depth of their understanding. People also forget what they bring to the table during job interviews or sales pitches. Similarly, boxers sometimes forget just how good they are in those final few hours before battle. The minute people engage in self-questioning, they become trapped inside of themselves and then, victims of their own imprisonment.

As Muhammad Ali once said: "I am the greatest, I said that even before I knew I was". What you say to yourself and the language you choose to say it with will determine whether you are able to push forward and through your warm-up, emerging with a free mind, or whether you are trapped - paralyzed inside of your thoughts and fears. To free yourself, you have to take that next step and place faith in your abilities, your preparation, and your working team. There is no time like the present to go with what you've got. You will be doing that anyway: why not believe in it?

Many years ago, I sat alone in a dressing room with a boxer just before he was about to warm-up and fight to unify world titles against another world champion. The boxer was paralyzed with fear that he might lose all that gained to that point in his professional career.

As we sat there, I asked him whether anyone could deny him of his past accomplishments? In that moment, he relaxed, took control of his room, and started to shadow box. From there, he warmed into what became the best ever performance of his life. Though the bout, hosted in the opponent's hometown was judged a draw, there was little question that my client actually won that bout by a large margin. The thing is, fear of losing what one has makes no sense when one is looking to expand one's territory.

TUNING-UP

Tuning is all about those last little details that the contender needs to remember in advance of the battle. The reminders are very specific, built in relation to the challenge ahead, tailor made as the touchstone strategies that will carry the contender to victory.

These skills need to be at his fingertips and in the forefront of his mind from the very beginning of battle. In reviewing the customized skills very briefly, the contender remembers what he needs to remember.

As you can see, warming involves body and mind, but it also must narrow and become extremely specific in relation to the test ahead. You need to transition from warming to tuning your mind and body before you ever engage in that important performance. You need to be focused and radiating with the necessary amount of intensity. That intensity then comes across as charisma, confidence and readiness when the time comes to deliver your knockout punch.

Reminders from Your Corner

- When you walk into the performance environment, you need to look the part of a performer, with an assertive walk and a posture that suggests you mean business.
- You need to stretch and generally warm your body each day before going off to do battle. If you stretch correctly from head to toe, you will carry yourself correctly, feel fluid in your movement and look every part a champion.
- Near the end of the warming process, you need to free your mind and focus only on the job at hand. To do so, you must first acknowledge that your preparation was comprehensive, meaning that you garnered the skills necessary for the immediate battle.
- The tuning up process requires about twenty minutes to sharpen your skills. The skills to be sharpened must include the two or three items that will be most important in the battle ahead. Remember, tactics are always specific to the context you are about to engage in.
- Finally, knowing that you are ready, you must take that necessary leap of faith and let go.

STEP NINE: THE ENTRANCE

The dry ice rises from the ground, the arena has gone dark and the lights and cameras pan onto the contender. What will the people see? This is the beginning of a new moment where the contender steps forward into the light and advances onward to becoming a champion. The question is will he advance now that the moment has arrived? Some people choose to step forward where others sadly retreat. The contender's job is to step forward.

The entrance provides a strong indication of what is to come for the performer. He needs to steel himself for the task ahead and walk forward with conviction and certainty. The moment has come for the performer to make his move and bring his training to fruition through performance when it counts most – within the performance opportunity.

The entrance begins with the fighter's first step into the arena, progresses to the contender entering and then possession the ring, onward to his connection with his audience, and culminating with his locking eyes onto his adversary. The boxers I work with are always taught to walk to the ring entrance with purpose. There is no time to touch gloves with the public on the way to the ring or engage in a protracted ceremonious entrance. There is only one task to do – narrow attention onto the purpose ahead through a mean and lean walk.

At the best of times, my clients listen to my advice and make their entrance succinctly and with focus. Every boxer must stay warm during his entrance, and so his entrance must facilitate his readiness. There are also instances when clients haven't listened to me in regards to their entrance. Not long ago, one of my clients insisted on creating a long and drawn out entrance with rap singers, dry ice, and a prolonged appearance on a stage, in advance of his walk to the ring. Sadly, the boxer was off-focus by the time he arrived at the ring, and it cost him his world title. Indeed, he over-estimated the importance of making a show and under-estimated the importance of arriving in the ring, ready for battle.

My experience has been that the entrance strategy can build momentum toward a great performance, or it can replace the fight as the priority, and become the performance. The thing is, the performer must stay warm and focused during the entrance. All else is irrelevant when the opening bell sounds to engage in battle.

For most every performer, the entrance is all about impression management. Your goal is not to impress, but rather, to assert yourself and suggest that you are well armed for the test ahead. Knowing that you are ready, you have a level of confidence that transmits to those in front of you. Make every step and movement count with full impact. This chapter is all about the entrance you need to make in order to gain further advantage before you even start battling.

THE WALK

Within every performance setting there is some form of entrance. For the high profile boxer, the entrance is one of those moments where the athlete looks to gain a double dividend. On one level the walk to the ring and entrance provides a very valuable indication of whether the boxer is going to deliver the goods. Is he building focus? Is he walking with conviction? Does he appear to own the arena? Is his energy and facial expression positive, yet serious? Is his focus narrow? All of these questions provide a first, though accurate glimpse into exactly where the performer is in terms of mindset. If he does his job correctly, one dividend is gained through his self-confidence.

Concurrently, the micro-expressions of the boxer never lie – you can always find out exactly where the performer is at by watching his eyes, his mouth and his forehead. These telltale markers never lie. The objective is to make certain that every emotional expression is suggestive of confidence, conviction, and certainty. The second dividend, then, can be gained from what the opponent sees when looking at the contender. It is one thing to be confident several days before the battle. It is an entirely different task to be tough minded and focused when the moment of truth is upon him. From what the adversary sees in the contender his confidence should waver, building further confidence through indirect means – in the contender. The entrance means a lot; it is also that first blink impression, snapped by the people who already are judging the performance to come.

You need to remember that when you act with conviction, you are also perceived as having that X Factor people are looking for in a winner. Impression management indeed, softens up the opponent so that you can move in for the kill. To take full advantage of your entrance, be parsimonious in your entrance and only use as long as is needed to prepare yourself for battle. Look your opponent square in the eye and show only confidence and certainty in yourself. From what you reveal, your judges or opponents will gain confidence in you, to the point where you will start winning your battle before the bell is ever sounded to mark the start of the fight.

Owning the Ring

There is that first moment when the boxer lays foot in the ring. The first thing he should do is stretch down and touch the canvas with his gloves and then rise and take a deep breath right down to the depth of his belly. More often than not, nervous boxers deprive themselves of this crucial step and instead, take in a shallow first breath. When one lacks oxygen, one lacks self-control and clarity of thought. With shortness of breath, panic isn't far behind. Anxiety should not serve as the platform to performance. In sharp contrast, when the contender takes his deep breath, his first seconds in the ring are spent building further control, and from that control, confidence and clarity of thought. Where you end is often the end of product of where you begin.

When performers enter into their final few minutes before making their big pitch, they often times rob themselves of self-control. The basis of self-control starts with your breath and moves outward from there. You need to take a deep breath, down to the very bottom of your abdomen, pushing that air into the deepest recesses of your body. With extra air you will think clearly and find solutions and strategies that bring out all of your strengths and preparation.

Next, your task is to ensure that you continue to breath from your belly as you deliver your pitch. There are always signs of where you are in terms of the quality of your breathing. If you are yawning, it's time to take in a deep breath. Yawning is often the search for more oxygen via a deep breath. If you experience shortness of breath it means that you are chest breathing, and not taking in the amount of oxygen that you need to think on your feet. Performance is essentially easy to master and it comes from the most basic of strategies regardless of who you are and the challenge you are about to face.

Finally, you need to continue on your way to success with an open posture to really press your advantage. There is nothing worse physically than caving in your shoulders and tightening your rib cage. In sport we talk about athletes having "ring presence". To be at your best, you need to be assertive, and you need to feel assertive. When you open your posture, you will take one step closer to occupying the complete role of performer and imposing your stature upon your judges.

LOCKING EYES ONTO YOUR TARGET

Boxers are always amazed how different their opponents look when they view each other from across the ring. Part of how the boxer goes about growing himself is by locking eyes onto his target through an impenetrable gaze. The opponent is now the target, and so the contender never takes his eyes off his opponent from that moment onward to the end of the fight. The opponent is now within his crosshairs. The contender becomes a hunter and his champion becomes the hunted.

Not long ago, one of my clients was preparing to do battle with Bernard Hopkins – one of this century's iconic warriors. In advance of the fight, Hopkins' coach Nazim Richardson correctly pointed out during a press conference that my client would not truly understand what it's like to be in the ring with Bernard Hopkins until they were rising from their opposite stools in the ring, and the bell sounded to start the fight. Nazim went on to explain that at that moment, it would only be my client and Hopkins. Soon thereafter, the fight ensued and the result was a draw between these two great boxers. However, what was apparent during the fight was that Nazim was correct. Great champions have a look about them and they also have learned to gaze right through their opponents.

When a professional outside of sport looks at his challenge, whether it is an audience, an employer, or even an exam, he needs to focus his gaze on the task at hand and hold that gaze steady. As a former student, on the way outside from the exam hall after I finished writing, I sometimes noticed people still writing exams, though looking all over the exam hall as if they were searching for the answers outside of themselves. The reality is that the answer for every performer is always staring him or her right in the face. People need to engage with their challenge and use a hard focus and lock on to the test. There is no turning away from the challenge.

If the challenge is to impress an employer or hiring committee, again, the objective is to hold the gaze of your evaluators and let them know that you are the best choice, the only real contender. People can only judge what is right there in front of them. Promises are one thing and tangible behaviors are another. People need to see and feel the merchandise in order to really buy into the product, and so, "what they see becomes what they get" when the first bell sounds to start the battle.

LAST MINUTE STEELING

After the boxers touch gloves, they return to their respective corners and gather themselves for the fight. For the contender to move forward and catapult himself to greatness, he has to steel himself, meaning he has to grit his teeth and commit to the battle. It is impossible to wait in the corner for the sound of the bell, passively. The contender should feel like a caged animal about to be let loose on his prey. Now is the very second when the grit and determination of training has to be carried forward. There is a reason why the contender has suffered through blood, sweat and tears, and that reason needs to manifest into the present.

There is many a contender who looks great on paper, but what separates a great hope from a great hype in the game of high-level professional boxing is the willingness to grit one's teeth and bear down when the time comes to perform. So what does the boxer do to steel himself? He takes a good deep breath to the bottom of his abdomen and then focuses next on exactly what he needs to do during the first few seconds of battle. The only way to turn one's nerves to steel is to focus inward on the strategy and a resolute commitment to that strategy. The goal is to push the game plan forward and impose it slowly but surely on the opponent. Only one boxer can fully exert his strategy, and that boxer must be the real contender. As Mike Tyson once proclaimed: "I'm scared every time I go into the ring, but it's how you handle it. What you have to do is plant your feet, bite down on your mouthpiece and say, 'Let's go.'"

Last minute steeling is something we have all engaged in at one point or other during our lives, when face to face with a challenge. Last minute steeling is something we all can do and yet few of us really push ourselves forward when the time comes. There is a tendency in each of us to fight or fly away. The steeling process is unique in that only one option is considered at that very moment – to fight one's fight.

Fight might not mean what some take it to be literally. Some strategies require fancy footwork where others require a linear - forward approach where you take the fight to the opponent. The strategy you have chosen for your fight is in part determined by the test you will face and not just by your own personality. Your approach to battle has to match perfectly with who you are and what you are facing. When you steel yourself, you are simply touching base with what that strategy is and that no matter what you commit to pushing your plan forward until you break down your opponent's resistance.

Reminders from Your Corner

- It is one thing to look the part and an entirely other thing to be the part. When you step into the ring you need to be the part and grow your stature by standing tall.
- When you step onto the platform to perform, take a deep breath and fill your abdomen to its very depth. A full abdomen of air will lead to clear thinking and good decisions.
- Only one person can own the arena. You need to take possession of the stage and give it up to no one. When you stand on the platform if you feel like you own it, you will also feel in control, make good decisions, and become an influential performer.
- Once you have taken your deep breath, lock your eyes onto the opponent. The opponent is your target audience and you need to grab his or her attention. Always keep your eyes of the opponent, that person is your target.
- Take the last few seconds before battle and gather yourself together. Push yourself to focus on what needs to be done in the fight and then commit to that plan from the split second the first bell sounds to mark Round One.

STEP TEN: ON FIRE BUT THINKING

When the bell sounds to mark the start of the fight, the first glimpse of truth about the fighters is revealed. Everything before the fight is meant to build momentum and conviction, but the acid test in terms of who goes forward and who backs up can only be revealed when the two fighters engage in battle.

Inside the ring the two boxers realize much sooner than do the spectators what fight they are in for. As Joe Louis stated: "Once that bell rings you're on your own. It's just you and the other guy." Some initial glimpses might indicate the contender is more than ready for the challenge he now faces or that he is in for the fight of his life. Regardless of what the contender's first blink impression is, in reality many extremely promising contenders begin the fight strong, become far too comfortable, only to realize too late there has been a reversal of fortune, with the momentum in the fight having shifted to his opponent.

Many years ago when I was an up and coming elite amateur athlete I heard the phrase "on fire but thinking" as a means of capturing what has to be done by the aspiring champion when he is in the heat of battle. What the term represents is a commitment to intensity from the first bell, with that intensity directed strategically as part of a larger battle plan. Some prospects believe being on fire is enough to win every battle, but they realize far too late that fire without its counterpoint of ice, only permits for a one dimensional and predictable battle plan.

Even when the contender sees opportunities, and even when things are going perfectly, he needs to stay within his strategy and take his sweet time. There might be time deeper into the fight when the contender needs to throw caution to the wind, but that time has not yet arrived. The struggle, then, is an internal one, where the contender needs to stay patient, even when people from the audience are urging him to finish off the opponent prematurely. The importance of staying within his body and his plan are everything in terms of the final outcome.

Passion is an important part of one's delivery, but so too are logic and patience. Opponents need to be softened up before the performer lands that telling - final punch, or series of punches. The softening up of opponents sometimes takes only a few rounds and sometimes it requires an entire bout to close the show and end in victory. If you are to move from contender to champion, you need to stay within your plan and take all the time you need in order to close the show. Getting to the finish line prematurely, you might deliver too much information too soon. You might, in a sense, punch yourself out (i.e. punch too early to the point of exhaustion). Your job is to bide your time, soften up your opponent and when the time is right, and only when the time is right, move in for the kill. This chapter is about how to balance the fire in your emotions with the coolness of your mind so that you will produce a complete performance – ending in a compelling win.

USING THE RING'S PARAMETERS

The parameters of the ring vary with each bout. Its dimensions are usually set by the champion; with the contender required to fight within its confines. When the champion decides on the size of the ring, he chooses between a large ring so that he can move laterally and use his footwork, downward to a small ring where he can pressure the contender and leave the contender with nowhere to seek refuge.

What many a fading or overly simplistic champion doesn't realize is that the contender, also, can use the full territory of the ring, meaning every square foot, to his advantage. A few years ago, I worked with a contender who was fighting a supposedly dangerous world champion. It was abundantly clear leading up to the fight the champion and his working team anticipated a blow out of a mentally weak contender. No matter what the contender said leading up to the fight, they all smirked.

Then came the first bell. The champion launched forward in his strategy to overcome the contender. When that very thing happened, the champion found the contender somewhere else – somewhere to the right or left of him. The champion reset his effort each time, and with each effort, he was once more denied access to the contender. Before long the bout looked like the exchange between a bull (the champion) and a matador (the contender). The champion became a mad dog, and the contender became the dog whisperer.

The bout was for the most part uneventful for the contender, only because he tempered his enthusiasm with a commitment to his team's strategy. When he needed to move, he moved. Sometimes he won the early rounds by scoring a single blow, which was in sharp contrast to the champion's inability to catch up with the contender. Other times the contender brought the champion to the center of the ring and exchanged blows at close range. Every decision in terms of where to go in the ring was made by the contender and before long, it became abundantly clear to the champion and his working team that they were followers in every aspect of the exchange. The momentum shifted early in favor of the contender and he never gave up that momentum. The end result was a unanimous decision and crowning of a new king and a new era.

The reason for that shift in performance traces largely to a strategy taught to the contender and the rest of his team by a new coaching staff member. The strategy was to perform using a diamond shape – staying away from the dangerous corners of the ring. When you think about most poor performances in high-end boxing, they happen on the ropes and in the corners when the weaker or less focused fighter is backed up, trapped and helpless. The opposite to being trapped is never to have one's back against the ropes.

The ring is yours to use and the strategies you take in the early moments of your battle need to include a wide number of different tactics, conceived to tame your opponent.

Many a performer forgets that even in a square box there is lots of room to move, so long as one uses not only the perimeter, but also, the entire geographic area in the box. Fights are won and lost on battle fields all of the time. Some pugilists adhere to conventional rules and only see the battlefield perimeter. Others can see things more globally as if their minds are hovering above the battlefield, playing a game of chess. The bottom line is that even when someone else sets the perimeter of a battle field, so long as you stay within its ropes, there is lots of space to move laterally, fake out your opponent, score your blows and then move out of range from the opponent.

When you engage in battle, you need to understand the full geography available to you. Just because others might not consider the complete geography available throughout the battle, does not mean you should be limited in what geography you might use. You need to understand in advance of the battle all of the geography open to you and then during the fight, take the opponent into uncharted territory – where you are familiar, and she/he, unfamiliar.

Final Adjustments

There is always a general idea of what will happen in the fight, and if the contender is well prepared his sense of what he will see in front of him should be quite accurate. However, even when things are pretty much as the contender anticipated them, there are still some minor adjustments that need to happen in the first round. These minor adjustments are crucial adaptations to the environment and how the contender is to perform in that environment.

Great boxers need to adjust to their environments and nowhere are those adjustments more salient than in the first few moments of battle, when there are slight uncertainties. After all, there is a distinct difference between knowing of an opponent and then knowing that opponent first-hand. Some promising boxers are great so long as things go their way. Greatness happens when the boxer sees or senses something unfamiliar and refines his strategy in relation to the challenge he now faces. The capacity to adjust, then, is what separates "great" from "good", in a moment when the boxer needs great.

The decision to make minor adjustments and then implement those adjustments provides the contender with a level of confidence that puts him right over the top, where he showcases his talents. In high profile boxing, even in the best and most exciting of fights, one boxer is better able to adjust to what is in front of him and the other lags behind. Adjustments are a necessary part of what the contender must bring to the table early on, before he formalizes his bout plan. The contender needs to understand and be willing to refine his strategies at the very beginning of the battle to slowly gain traction and then press forward his advantages over a rigid opponent.

When it is time to start the battle, there is always a sort of feeling out process early on. The information you gain through that process can guide you and provide you with the directional arrows of where you need to go. Curves in the road require an adjustment to your navigation so that you can literally stay on track. When people go off track during a performance they can lose sight of where they are and become completely disoriented in terms of where to go next and of equal importance, how a decision in the present can link with overall success.

Adjustments to your strategy are a critical part of what you need to do in the heat of battle. Nothing is predictable and questions or challenges can come out of the woodwork very early on. You need to refine who you are and to a small degree, what you are doing in order to keep pace in the performance early on. When you are able to respond and refine your strategies, you will hone in and target excellence in the midst of performance. Those who will be watching and judging you will see your capacity to adjust, and rest assured, they will be impressed. Flexibility always trumps rigidity.

Going to the Body

The best boxers often need to be softened up before they are taken down. There are boxers who are dangerous with one punch, but many of the best boxers today take down their opponents through punch volume. In a well-formed strategy, some of the best boxers on the world scene are excellent body punchers at the beginning of the fight. The reason why is because body punches slow down the opponent and take away his legs, his oxygen and his resistance so he cannot escape the onslaught of an assault through fancy footwork.

Going to the body is something the contender needs to do very early on. The punches he invests going to the body do not immediately show up in terms of opponent weakness. Going to the body takes time and the damage accumulates. When the contender embarks on the process of body punching at the very beginning of the fight, eventually his opponent weakens, becomes winded and then lowers his hands to protect his ribcage. At that very moment the opponent's his chin is exposed and vulnerable to the knockout punch.

Many performers look for that knockout punch at the very beginning of the performance. Perhaps early on in her or a career, people will be impressed by that one big idea or action. As the performer claws up to the pinnacle of the profession, things become different. The judging is much more stringent and people are not easily impressed by a correct decision or strategy. Judges of your performance, be they employers or other types of consumers of your ideas, will need to be chipped away at a little at a time, from the very beginning. Experienced judges need to be softened up before they eventually give way and conceded your greatness.

I recall how I began my consulting in boxing. I was working as a low level administrator for the Canadian Olympic Committee, at the 1996 Summer Olympics. I always wanted to work with boxing and before long I found my entry point. I identified the Technical Director for the Canadian National Boxing Team, a good friend of mine to this day, and kept bringing him coffee until he noticed me. I persisted to the point where we would meet for coffee each afternoon and hang out. When I returned home after the Olympics I phoned him relentlessly each week until he gave me a chance to work with the Canadian National Junior Boxing Team. The rest was history. Had I not chipped away at my new friend with lots of small body shots, so to speak, he would never have relented. There were others who failed before me because they were looking to land that one knockout punch that would impress him at the start of a discussion. The reality is that more times than not, good successes require time and persistence.

The Plan in Motion

There comes a point early on in the fight when the contender knows exactly what is in front of him. To this point he has tested his opponent, thrown punches from different angles, re-tested his opponent's reflexes and from the information he has gained, formalized his refined plan. He knows the soft spots of his opponent and those are the places he is going to go while imposing his strategy.

In every fight there is always one boxer who arrives at his strategy faster. Some of the reason for his quick calibration stems from an earlier profiling and customized training in relation to his adversary. The rest of the reason for his quick arrival at a plan in the ring is explained by his ability to refine that strategy and adjust himself in accordance with the adversary he is facing that very night.

The best performances in life come from being the leader. There are cues in the environment about what works and what doesn't work. All you need to do is look for the micro-expressions of your opponent(s). From his eyes alone you will see what he is open to and what strategies create a strong resistance on his part. Your opponent, in turn, can be won over very quickly providing you choose to test him with a diversity of attempts, learn what you need to learn from his cues, and then move forward with some very important targeting information that aligns with what he is looking for.

Presenters sometimes struggle from information overload. They might see glimpses of the informational cues given by their audience, but they become passive to those cues. Because there can only be one leader, when the performer becomes passive, he relinquishes the stage to his audience and so, his judges. The performer's fate is then in the hands of others, much like an opponent who is visibly on the losing end of an exchange. Because there can only be one leader, no matter what, as a performer, you need to take the lead, take in the important cues from your opponent and then use those cues to your advantage. Knowing your opponents, you can lead them to exactly where you wish to take them.

REMINDERS FROM YOUR CORNER

- We all must perform in the confines of a ring with four sides and stay inside the ropes. Many people perform use only the perimeter of the ring and execute their punches from the outside. Even the smallest ring has many square feet of uncharted geography that you could use to execute your plan. Punch and move using the ring's entire geography.
- Even with the best-formed strategies there are always minor adjustments that you need to make to your game plan, especially at the beginning of the performance. It is one thing to know your opponent well, a slightly other thing to experience him first-hand in the heat of battle.
- Success at the top level requires a body punching strategy where you land smaller punches that over time break down your opponent's resistance. Wins are often the result of an accumulation of good decisions.
- Your audience has soft spots in their armor – ideas they are enthused by. Look carefully at what they are telling you through their expressions and watch for their cues before you refine your battle strategy.

Step Eleven: Hit Below the Belt

Battles rarely go perfectly and entirely according to the plan. Sooner or later there will be a moment where the performer is hit below the belt. Surprise or dirty punches seem to come out of nowhere and they can quickly reverse the contender's momentum. For many a boxer, the punch below the belt is paralyzing and takes his focus away from strategy and redirects it to the pain he is feeling. At that very moment, the opponent has the contender exactly where he wants him – off focus.

When boxers prepare for crucial bouts, there is a tendency to prepare for optimal performance and to overlook the unpredictability that will happen when the opponent seeks to regain the advantage. The unknown can be paralyzing when it happens, and it is virtually impossible to predict exactly how the opponent might go about taking the contender off focus. The punch might be in the form of an illegal blow behind the head or below the belt. Regardless what dirty tact is used, there are ways to respond that return the contender to focus and the advantage earned up to that point.

In your life, you can expect that sooner or later, a person or circumstance will unfold that will catch you by surprise. The question is not whether you will get hit by a dirty punch in a crucial moment, but rather how you will handle the dirty punch after the fact. Will you be paralyzed, so much so that you won't get off the canvas in time to beat the count? Will you jump up too quickly, before you recovered from the punch? Will you lose complete emotional control and enter into a blind rage, all fire, no ice? Or, will you take just enough time to get your feet back from under you, and then resume control over your opponent? The decision is yours to make how you wish to respond to the dirty tactics of trench warfare, and it requires good judgment, clarity of thought, discipline, and mental toughness.

Just as much, if not more, can be learned about you in moments of adversity as in moments when things are going according to your plan. To really win your environment over, you need to have both sets of skills. Getting hit below the belt can test your resolve and also your capacity to scratch and claw your way to glory. You need to embrace hard moments when nasty setbacks happen, learn what you need to learn very quickly, and then re-assert yourself as the contender you really are. There is nothing wrong with moments that test character and everything right in your desire to bounce back. This chapter targets the unforeseen setbacks that you will experience in life as a result of dirty tactics from your opponents, and how to battle back from those setbacks with determination and solid focus.

USING THE EIGHT COUNT

When a boxer is in trouble, the referee steps in and administers an eight count. The eight count provides the boxer with a stay of execution so he can get his breath, regroup and get back on his feet with stability. The reprieve of a few seconds is all the time the boxer can afford without conceding defeat. Some of the best boxers have not learned the value in an eight count, the allotted time is often all that he needs to regroup, that is, providing he uses the count to regroup mentally and physically before returning to action.

Just a few weeks ago, I witnessed a boxer on the edge of greatness. He was fighting a lesser opponent, and the success of the opponent was all that separated him from a multi-fight deal with the largest sport television network. The opponent was wiser than the contender gave him credit for. The opponent chipped away at the contender and started coming on mid-way through the fight. The opponent also understood what opportunities were just beyond the immediate fight. In Round Seven the contender was caught with a punch to his temple and for the first time in his life, his legs were wobbly. The referee correctly stepped in and started the count and instead of the contender taking a knee and regrouping, he remained on his feet.

Now, taking a knee is in many instances the correct strategy when one's legs are shaky. Despite boxers understanding the value in taking a knee, several of the most promising and talented of boxers forget to do so in the heat of battle, when they find themselves in trouble. Sometimes eight seconds is all that is needed to regain footing. With their feet back under them, those who use their head can re-establish themselves and go on to victory. Sadly, the contender I just spoke of made the wrong decision, returned to battle a few seconds too early, and shortly afterward his corner threw in the towel. The fight was over, and so was the contender's possibility of becoming the world champion and a multi-millionaire.

In stark contrast, I have worked with one amazing boxer, who in advance of his first world title opportunity, understood that he was about to encounter a champion with dirty tactics. When the contender was hit by a punch behind the head early on in the bout, he retaliated with a few illegal punches of his own, after he took the necessary time to recover. He matched dirty tactics with dirty tactics. The contender understood that he was in for a war. He took the necessary time to recover, and met the champion on level ground through dirty tactics of his own.

In trench warfare, you will be hit below the belt or stung by a punch that will leave you shaken, sooner or later. The dirty punch might be in the form of a nasty or misleading question during a job interview or a virtual attack on your credibility by someone you work with. How you act in that moment will define whether you regroup and get yourself back into the game, or not. You need to take a knee from time to time and allow yourself those valuable few seconds to get your feet back under you. In contrast, it is virtually impossible to battle back when your thinking and reflexes are still reacting to the previous blow.

The few seconds to catch your breath is a lifeline – take it! The focus in those few seconds needs to be not on where you just came from, but instead, where you need to go from here to regain your control over your opponent. Take a deep breath first and then ask yourself the simple question "where to from here"? By forcing yourself to look ahead, you will automatically turn away from the problem and redirect your focus to solution oriented thinking. There is a reason why motivational consultants encourage their clients to look ahead in the heat of battle, just after a setback. A positive immediate future can only happen when you see it and once more start taking baby steps toward the possibility of success.

FIGHTING BACK

There comes a point when the contender needs to re-start his engine and throw punches. Activity and engagement are the only way back into the fight. The judges need to see him fight his way back into the fight one way or another. Mike Tyson has a famous quote that "everyone has a plan until he gets hit". To his statement you should understand the mentally toughest of fighters have a plan for after they get hit, also! Great boxers can scratch and claw their way back into a fight when all hope is lost and the immediate future looks bleak. Great boxers find a way to win where most others fold up their tent and save themselves for another day, taking the loss along the way.

Not that a loss is bad for the boxer. Some boxers learn a significant amount from a loss and come back even stronger from that point onward. However, the most important thing a great boxer requires is will, will to fight on, will to win, and the will to close the show. So, when faced with a setback, the best contender will get back onto his feet and then re-engage.

Being a contender means that you are built of strong stuff. Especially when your success is on the line and you are backed up against the ropes, you need to keep throwing punches. Eventually your opponent will back off and stay away from the range of your blows. Those punches might be in terms of ideas you want to sell, that others are initially not receptive to. The antics of your opponent might include hostility. If you can provide logic when answering each question as it is posed, no matter how nastily the question is framed you will eventually win over your opponent.

Success, then, is not only a matter of imposing yourself upon your opponent. It is also a matter of re-imposing. Fights are a matter of give and take. Famous warriors such as former great champion Arturo Gatti are known to take many punches during their epic battles, against profound opponents such as Mickey Ward, the boxer spoken of in the movie "The Fighter". Sometimes one must get dirty and battle back from the clutches of defeat, simply by throwing punches where others typically would wilt under adversity.

Relentless Focus

It is one thing to fight one's way back into the fight. Many boxers with heart do so regularly throughout each and every high level battle during their careers. The thing about fighting back is it takes the contender back into the fight, but it can also make the exchange a street fight and not a skilled boxing match. Boxing is not just about banging away at the opponent. Boxing is also a matter of stepping back, moving to the side, slipping punches, using skilled footwork, and throwing punches that gain one the advantage mentally and physically.

Not long ago, one of my clients who was a contender, fought in a world title bout against a skilled and more experienced opponent. The bout was going extremely well through the first four of twelve rounds. In round five my client became over confident after he sent his adversary, the champion, to the canvas, much to the surprise of the crowd. Not thirty seconds later his opponent punched him behind the head and in the next exchange when my client was unfocused, landed a punch to his temple that left my client wobbly in his legs. He survived the round and when the television panned to his facial expression in the corner, it was perfectly clear that his thought process was "right, that was sloppy, never again". From rounds six through twelve he fought with intelligence and a solid defense, onward to an epic world title.

Once the contender has fought his way back into the fight, his job is to return to boxing. One of the crucial lessons he needs to keep in the back of his mind after his wake-up call, having been hit with a dirty punch, is that he needs to be on guard and focused on his defense as much as his offense. Many a boxer has won rounds in a critical bout by landing only one punch in the round. When the opponent's offense is nullified to no scoring blows, one punch is all that the contender needs to take the round from the champion.

After any wake-up call, when a performer gets her or his feet stabilized, performance has to be shifted from brawling and heart onward to strategic fighting and a relentless focus. In an argument, debate, or the selling of an idea to a prospective buyer, there will be times when you will be caught off guard and need to thrash your way back into performance. There will also be a time when you are back in control and your communication strategy will need to be modified back to a soft sell, with points pulled into your selling, strategically. Your goal is not to bash a consumer or adversary over the head once that person has relented. At a certain point you need to return to your plan and lead that person or group of people where you want to take them to go. Your job is then to bank rounds and work towards a win, all the while being nimble on your feet just in case a second foul comes your way.

REMINDERS FROM YOUR CORNER

- When you get hit with a surprise, dirty blow, take a few seconds and regroup. You need that few seconds to catch your breath, regain your balance and to think forward in terms of where to go from that point.
- When you return to battle, you need to throw punches and regain some control by backing off your opponent. No matter what you do, keep throwing punches and if you do, you stand a good chance of scratching and clawing your way back into the fight.

- Once you have regained control, temper your enthusiasm and remain sharp. Throw your punches strategically and be prepared for the next dirty punch that might come your way. Better to be prepared with a good defense than caught a second time.

Step Twelve: The Championship Rounds

Until a contender enters into a championship fight, the number of rounds for his battles could vary from four to ten. Fights are always shorter when there is less at stake. At a certain point, though, every contender needs to move on to a twelve round fight as he seeks a championship belt. The extended length of fight is not for the faint of heart. Until a fighter has been in a twelve round fight he will never know just how much stamina he really has. It takes lots of gas in the tank to be at one's best for twelve rounds.

Rounds eleven and twelve are what separate the men from the boys. It is relatively easy to grit one's teeth when there is still some energy and coordination in reserve. It is an entirely other matter to fight to the point of exhaustion – to the bottom of one's own self. I have witnessed many a client reach the bottom of his endurance in these final two rounds. When the contender is running on fumes and at the bottom of his energy stores; that is when we find out whether he has adequate makings of a champion. Several of the most successful boxers have completed twelve rounds, given their all, and then required oxygen and medical assistance when seeking to catch their breath, lower their heart and regain their physical and psychological control. It is one thing to observe an epic battle of twelve rounds on television and an entirely other matter to go twelve rounds successfully, one's self.

When I speak about the championships rounds, the term obviously extends beyond boxing to life challenges that will take you to the very bottom of your stamina. When you push toward the pinnacle of your career or prepare to pass a board exam, or a graduate degree, the championship rounds pertain to the inevitable exam you must take. Law entrance exams often consume a full day, which is equivalent to twelve rounds of boxing. A doctoral dissertation defense often lasts for three or more hours, where the student is required to think on her or his feet every minute throughout the entire process. Job interviews in an academic setting sometimes require two full days of the candidate.

On all counts, one slip can leave the high achiever gasping for breath. The championship rounds relate to the time in your performance when you are exhausted and your concentration is on the verge of decline. You will never know what it is like to gather yourself together and push through that exhaustion to the other side, and success, until you fight your own epic twelve round battles.

You will have several epic battles to fight in your lifetime. What you need to do in those instances is somehow, no matter what, "gut it out" and persist until the final bell. There is no telling when in the final two rounds you will overtake your opponent and win the battle. This chapter tackles the championship rounds and what needs to be done in order for you to become the champion.

DIGGING DEEP

No boxer ever really knows what he is made of until he reaches into the depths of himself in terms of physical and mental stamina. Many a boxer on the precipice of greatness has fallen short in the final two rounds of a championship fight, only to lose a close decision that was decided, even in the final fifteen seconds. The thing is that greatness knocks at each of our doors only a few times in a lifetime, and sometimes opportunities come in the eleventh hour. Should he choose to step forward during this formative moment in his epic battle, what he will gain through the experience is unparalleled confidence and self-knowledge. On the other hand, when the choice is made to leave success in the hands of the judges and not to finish with conviction, the contender sets a career pattern for himself that only takes him to the precipice of greatness, where he can almost touch it, but not grasp it.

Several years ago, I was asked to work with a very promising professional boxer. He was highly capable of becoming a world champion. The one barrier that separated him from greatness was his lack of belief in his own stamina. The boxer was an accomplished amateur boxer with the capacity to excel in professional boxing. Sadly, in his first opportunity to fight for a world title, he faded in the final few rounds against an eminent opponent. The bout that followed confirmed a pattern of performance of fading in the final few rounds, despite all of the athletic ability in the world. At the culmination of the boxer's career, he fought for three world titles, always coming close, but never succeeding.

The person who finds another gear and is able to look beyond immediate exhaustion and see that victory is the more likely of the two boxers to succeed. It is quite a challenge to step through exhaustion and bank rounds where others look within themselves only to realize that what they are confronting is pain and hardship. There is immediacy in the decision to find another gear or stall out in one's performance. If only every capable boxer would realize the fatigue and pain of the moment is transient and fleeting.

We all get pushed to the brink at some point in our career and even in our personal lives. You need to push through the walls of internal resistance and come out the other side a changed person. When you challenge yourself, battle with fatigue, disregard that fatigue, and step forward, you are likely to surpass most every other employee in your workplace and also in your larger profession. Many people just don't want to pay the price for success when a price must be paid. If you want to be a standalone, you need to go places in your body and mind that others just won't go. The air is thin at the top, and hard to breath. Just the same, you need to acclimate yourself and keep breathing – even when you are gasping for oxygen.

Finding Another Gear

When the contender pushes through exhaustion, he is actually surprised to find another gear he never knew existed. Every boxer who described this experience to me spoke of a period of time in the later rounds where he felt he was bottoming out. In that moment he decided to give the bout his all no matter what. Expecting to fade, these boxers actually reached another level in their stamina and found they could go much further. Once a boxer decides to push himself onward to discomfort, through that discomfort, and onward to excellence, he frees himself from inhibition and fear and looks to repeat the experience time and time again. When one looks at the great world champions in boxing one finds a person willing to search for and then find another gear. In so doing, he finds more depth in himself than he ever knew existed.

We all have another gear, if only we would look for it. We are surrounded by many employees, often unwilling to push through exhaustion, onward to greatness. People love to be comfortable, and often hate breaking a sweat, let alone going well beyond that point! The sad consequence for most people is that they never realize their potential. People, far too quickly, assume they only have one gear. The reality is that you have many gears. All you need to do is step on the clutch, shift the gear, and then step on the accelerator. You need to stretch yourself and push through discomfort in order to achieve new boundaries in performance.

Don't expect to find support as you seek to find this new gear inside of yourself. Most people opt not to look for it, and would prefer that you do the same. How possibly could such people understand your quest for excellence? More likely, you will be told to relax, not exert yourself, and enjoy life. Several years ago, I was told by a senior colleague after an extraordinary academic year to slow down and relax. In response, I doubled my efforts and became a Canada Research Chair. Life is never more enjoyable than when you shift gears and take your pursuits to the next level. Few would understand your decision to find another gear, but then again, champions are few and far between.

CLOSING THE SHOW

Boxers always talk about fighting to the bell. Not long ago, I worked with a client defending his world title. He won the first ten of twelve rounds convincingly. In the eleventh round he began to fade, but was still able to hold off his opponent. He was hanging in part way through the twelfth round when in the last thirty seconds he was caught off guard by a well-placed punch by his opponent. My client went down to the canvas and just managed to beat his eight count. Just as the opponent was about to close the show, the bell sounded to mark the end of the fight.

From my client's vantage, he just barely escaped a catastrophe. From the opponent's, if he would have persisted just one percent more in the closing minute of the bout, he would have become the new world champion. The lesson for both athletes is that neither closed the show, and the result was contentious. Champions are made from maximum exertion from beginning to end. Those who take the fight to their opponents do so with full effort and commitment. More often than not, it is these people who really seal the deal and cap off a win with a convincing close to the fight.

I mentioned earlier on there is such a thing in social psychology as a "recency effect". Recency suggests when people are making a decision on an outcome just after having watched the performance, what stays with them is the performance as a whole, but in terms of each round, especially the last twenty to thirty seconds. It is these final images that seem to sway judges and leave a lasting impression when it comes time to score the round. Closing the show requires that the contender never take for granted the outcome of the fight – even in the last few seconds.

When you are performing to your utmost and the delivery of your ideas is just perfect, even then, you need to seal the deal through a flurry of punches and activity. The worst thing you can do is end off with a lasting impression of having faded down the stretch. Those who will judge your performances and be your gate keepers will look, as much at your persistence and stamina, as they will your overall performance.

It is often counter-intuitive to keep performing when you know you have a performance in the bag. Champions in the making do things that are unconventional and beyond the standards of less persistent people. If you are a student, the way you answer that last question can put you over the top and onward to a higher letter grade. If you are being interviewed for a new and more challenging position, typically those who are evaluating you will make their decision shortly after you leave the room. Make your closing argument compelling. If you are a sales person, your closing is just as important as your opening, largely because people open their wallets, not based on what you said in the middle of your pitch. Their impulse decision to buy what you are offering up is decided, often in the blink of an eye, just after you have ended your pitch. The bottom line is that you need to close the show in order to take the step forward to championship status.

Reminders from Your Corner

- If you want to be a champion you need to look within yourself and perform through exhaustion. Exhaustion is actually your friend because it lets you know that you are really exerting maximum effort.
- People have many more gears than they ever use. Most people live their lives in first gear. Dare to be different, push through fatigue, and find out that you are made of many gears, not just one.
- To be a true champion you need to build your momentum throughout the fight and then close with a bang. There is no telling whether your final effort will become the tipping point in your favor.
- The people who will judge your championship performance will always remember most what they see in the final fifteen seconds of a

round. Be certain to leave a lasting impression at the end of each and every round, especially during the championship rounds.

Step Thirteen: Crowning the New Champion

For those contenders who fight their way through to the very top, the reward that awaits them is a coronation. There are only a few crowned champions at one time, and these people have arrived at the pinnacle of the sport. Some stay as champions for a short period and are defeated in their next battle, others last for several years before being dethroned, and still others retire as undefeated champions.

What all of these people hold in common is that at one time or another, they are crowned as a king. In the immediate, each king has the opportunity to bask in his glory of greatness. After much work, he has finally realized his potential on paper, and moved beyond contender status to tangible champion. In those very moments, the king's response to his new found crowning determines just how long his reign lasts. Every little decision, especially those he decides to make under the microscope of success, provides an exact indication of where he is at mentally, and also where he is already starting to move next.

Some kings hoard the glory for themselves and do not appreciate the decisions they and their working team have made each step along the way. Such people in that moment start down a path of superficiality; living exclusively in the moment. Though it is a challenge while basking in the glory of success to look beyond the victory to a larger picture, great champions do exactly that. Almost immediately after they have achieved success, they step back for a second, consider those who've helped them along the way, and then turn their attention onto their next target. Champions never sleep. They cannot sleep – there are always contenders moving up the ranks.

Championship status is not a static achievement where one has "finally made it" and "arrived". There is no such thing as an arrival, only an ongoing pursuit toward excellence. Champions must continue to push the envelope, always, even when they have just achieved greatness. The very moment that they are celebrating is also a moment closer to their next epic battle. How a champion decides to spend that moment must in part tie back to where he wishes to go next.

There will be times in your life where you will fight for a championship of some sort or other. Each title is an accomplishment, but also a possible step forward to a next level. There is no end to the levels of opportunity and accomplishment you can achieve through your life path. In this chapter we will consider what needs to happen immediately after you have been crowned a champion.

Introducing the New King

The moment arrives when it is official and the champion is introduced to the audience and judges as king. So, how should he act in his moment of coronation? Remember, the words that leave his mouth start him on the path to his next battle. It is one thing to become a king, and an even tougher challenge to stay as king and progress forward from that first moment of greatness, using it as a platform for a higher level of greatness.

The champion must step up to the microphone while those around him are cheering and enthralled by his arrival at the top. In that very moment, the champion must look inward and speak from the depth of his heart and soul. If he does so, he sees not only his own success, but also the people around him. Successes are to be shared with his working team and also with his fans. This is his moment to be gracious, humble, and so, a person of substance.

In terms of his working team the champion knows that the championship title is not his, alone. His working team has served as generals in the trenches each step along the way, onward to this momentary success. Each member needs to be acknowledged, not only in name, but also for her/his contribution. In doing so, the champion steps forward with perspective, while at the same time valuing each member of his team as an important piece of the larger title: champion.

There are many champions that are champions on paper, who even then, cannot fill an arena. How is it a champion cannot garner the support of fans? Is it a matter of their abilities, or is it something in the way they carry themselves? There are many champions who are lesser boxers, but have a tremendous fan base. The audience is equivalent to oxygen for the boxer.

When they are there for the champion, they support him through thick and thin. They also can inspire him during the depths of battle, in those seconds when he is exhausted and searching for meaning. Now is him opportunity to give back and balance the scales.

When it comes to successes, no one accomplishes excellence in a vacuum. We all succeed as a result of our own hard work, but also through the assistance and efforts of those who've supported us each step along the way to championship status. Those who decide the moment they are crowned to accept all of the recognition alone have started down a path of loneliness, and at the same time, severed their connection to the human resources needed to push forward from one level of championship status to the next.

The greatest of champions realize very quickly that making it is a relative term. In every work setting, there are more accomplished people and less accomplished people. Even among those who are leaders in their workplace, should such people compare themselves against others at the top of their domain, they will realize very quickly that there is always a next level – a bigger foe. The step forward to the next level requires a mobilized effort with your working team supporting you onward to uncharted territory.

There must also be recognition your support comes from a much wider cast of characters than just your working team. There are family and friends, and all of the people who've wished you well during the various steps in your journey. The important thing to realize is their support needs to be retained as you go forward to the next level in your development. The support you've gained to this point will become that much more important as the stakes rise.

THE CALLING OUT

The transition forward to your next target happens very quickly, even within the first fifteen minutes after you've achieved a momentous win. After a world championship bout, while still in the ring, the boxer turns his attention to the commentator who is asking "where to from here"? The response from the boxer is termed a "calling out". At that very moment, the boxer considers his options and hopefully sets his sights on an opponent who will bring him to his next level. There are many more champions on paper than there are true world champions. The champion's goal must now be to move forward and onward to what is termed "lineal world champion". The lineal world champion is the big fish in a big pond – the champion among champions.

When asked who the champion wants to face next, already knowing the answer even before the recent battle, he turns his sights to a bigger and more established fish, meaning another world champion. He wishes to be the king of kings, and not just royalty perched on a thrown, with only a small territory to rule. The response comes without hesitation and with this step the boxer quickly understands that he must re-engage quickly through hard work in order to unseat a better-established champion.

Every height you reach opens you up to new and more inspiring opportunities. The objective is to continue looking forward into the horizon so that you could see the landscape in front of you and among that landscape, the territory you have yet to claim. Far too often, people in the workplace settle for good results at one level and fail to challenge themselves, onward to the next level. Every success opens you up to new opportunities and new heights. Success is a relative term, and also, it's not static. Dare to be different than those who surround you and push yourself beyond the protective cloak of a small lion, onward to a world where you are a king among kings.

The antithesis is a world champion who I met several times, some years ago. He became a world champion and to this day, remains a world champion in one of several world championship divisions. This champion is an undefeated boxer, but when one looks into his eyes, there no longer is the shine of a champion. He knows that he is being protected. The sad result is that his confidence is slowly fading, even though on paper he is a champion. Dare to be different and look beyond defending to extending your title to larger parcels of land.

Champagne and Opening up

The time comes to leave the ring and return t the comfort of the dressing room. The return to the dressing room is when the champion is greeted by all of his personal supporters, comprised of his working team, family and friends. People want to talk to the champion, shake his hand, pat his back, and snap photos with him and the newly acquired belt.

For the champion, this next part of the post-performance experience allows for celebration and also the opportunity to share in the spoils. As the champion is adjusting to his new title, and allowing the success to sink in, he also gains the opportunity to widen his focus. Celebrating is a group activity and a social event. It is the perfect foil and counter-point to the pre-bout routine when the boxer had to narrow his focus and close himself off from distractions.

Just as every performer needs to close off from distractions before a performance, there must also be a time to re-open to friends and family. Titles are not what keep us satisfied, in and of themselves. We need people, and to have them, we need to make space and time immediately after the victory. Friendships and social connections are something we need to cultivate, and what better time to do so then right after the big win? During that moment in time you need to acknowledge each the people sitting with you, and share the moment.

POST-BATTLE FATIGUE

The day after performance is typically the time when post-battle fatigue sets in for the new champion. When a boxer gives his all in a championship bout, his investment is much more than the previous evening's performance. There were twelve steps that I've outlined before the champion is crowned as a king. Each step has been overviewed in this book, and in several cases, a single step could take weeks or months to accomplish. What the steps represent is a tremendous investment in terms of time, one's body, mind, and emotions.

When the day post-performance arrives, the natural physical and emotional response is fatigue, alongside aches and pains. A post-performance emotional letdown period is an important part of the champion's natural life cycle. After a wave of success, there must also be some calm and quiet for the performer to regroup and then, surge once more. Emotional flatness is an important challenge as the boxer returns to the comfort, though also the quiet solitude and normal existence that people not engaged in high performance life live each day.

There is sometimes a tendency for recently crowned champions to sink into a series of behaviors that closely resemble episodic depression. The person is seen laying around the house and retreating into a quiet world. The boxer post-bout feels in limbo until the next target is identified and targeted, once more through training and pre-performance preparation. The danger in this pattern of retreating is that at some point in time, it will be time to step down as champion. What might one do then, retreat indefinitely? A vibrant approach to life opens the champion up to opportunities that might come her or his way at a random time. Champions are always ready to see the opportunities they come across, even those they encounter by coincidence. What separates a champion from any other boxer is his capacity to see each and every opportunity when he crosses paths with it.

You will also experience the highs and lows that a world champion boxer experiences. A high might be when you land a big contract, gain a sizeable salary increase, or complete a university degree. There needs to be a time to bask briefly in your accomplishment, and so too must there be a time to regroup and recharge. Vacations are a good way of physically forcing yourself into a break, all the while changing your physical scenery. Breaks are opportunities to do something new or something you have deferred while you were preparing for your challenge. During your break, regain the much-needed balance in your life. From there, you will more easily approach your next challenge with vigor.

Reminders from Your Corner

- There is a moment when the champion is introduced as "the new world champion". In that very moment, take the time to bask in the lights, but share those lights with your working team and also with the audience. You need both groups of people. When you are in the lights is exactly the right time to appreciate these people for who they are and what they've done for you.
- Great champions don't take long to call out their next target. Some of the best world champions call out their next opponent immediately after their success is proclaimed. Dare to keep re-setting your goals, and do so quickly after each big win.
- The post-performance success is best when shared with family and close friends. Take the time to enjoy the victory with the people who were there along the way. By doing so, you will automatically re-open yourself to your social connections.
- Post-bout fatigue is a natural part of every performer's life the day after an important fight. Take the time to regain balance and re-engage in activities that you gave up while in training.

Step Fourteen: Staying Mean, Staying Lean

One of the toughest challenges the champion will ever experience is to stay hungry once he's achieved his champion's status. There are many benefits to being a champion, including financial and social recognition. With praise and comfort, many a champion has let things slide and decreased his work ethic. Before long the lazy champion becomes soft and vulnerable to challenge from a fresh contender sharking his way up the ranks. It is only a matter of time before the comfortable champion is dethroned.

At the opposite end of the continuum, there are champions who feel tremendous pressure on their shoulders immediately after they achieved their champion's status. It is one thing to make it to the top and an entirely other thing to remain as champion. The minute one is crowned, one also becomes a target for contenders looking for their big break. There are only a handful of champions and it is quite a challenge to remain among the top seed.

The solution to any possibility of weakness is to stay mean and lean. The best champions continue to train with hunger regardless of what their status is. Belts are evidence that one is succeeding at the top, but what drives a champion is greatness in their skills. Champions seek to be the gold standard in their domain, and to dominate for a full tenure, not a fleeting moment. True boxing champions are no exception to the rule and always seek to expand their reach to a wider audience and a larger reputation.

There is only one way to build on the champion's status, and that is to return to the gym and go further in one's commitment to greatness. There can only be one moment when the boxer first becomes champion, but the status he's achieved opens much larger opportunities in the horizon. The status of champion is relative and the best seek to be the champion among champions. There is such thing as a pound for pound rankings list, where boxers across weight divisions are compared and contrasted. The goal is to be within the pound for pound rankings, moving closer to the top with each battle. True champions seek to be the cream of the crop.

There will come a time in your chosen performance area when you will be a title-holder. Your title might be mechanic, electrician, lawyer, psychologist, teacher, professor, master of business administration, or something else. It is wonderful to achieve the status of king in your working environment, but the pool of professionals in your area will be large. Once you have achieved greatness in a small pond, dare to swim in a larger one.

This chapter opens up a discussion about the things you need to do once you've become champion. The pillars to this step of performance are the need to look beyond your current status, and furthering your hunger through creativity and the recognition that bigger things are yet to come.

DEEP HUNGER

When a boxer is wired for performance and achieves that performance, one really finds out what that boxer is made of. Many years ago, I sat and listened to a world authority on intrinsic and extrinsic motivation, meaning motivation from within oneself versus motivation by external rewards such as fame and fortune. When a boxer becomes a world champion, money quickly follows. The rewards to several of my clients have been in the millions of dollars for one night's performance. Money and recognition tends to change the personality of many high-class champions for the worse. They tend to lose their focus. The question I asked the motivational guru was in cases when a boxer financially becomes wealthy, and is offered ever-increasing monetary reward, how can he maintain his intrinsic motivation? The response from the presenter was cold silence.

Many a boxer gets caught up in a glamorous lifestyle with flashy cars, expensive clothes, high-end jewelry, top-drawer alcohol, and all of the trappings of the wealthy. The gains of wealth are amazing and for some, they quickly become the focal point. Many a champion, once tasting the good life, progressively wants more luxury with each big win. The things that once motivated the boxer such as excellence and financial independence are no longer motivators. Life has changed, and for many that change is more than they can manage.

What separates the great champions from the rest is not only physical talent. What really puts great champions at the top of the sport is their pursuit of ongoing excellence. There are always technical aspects of the sport to improve, better tactics to be learned and also better team strategies. Perfection doesn't exist in professional boxing and there is no such thing as the perfect performance. The boxer needs to look within himself for an even deeper understanding of what makes him tick and then, how to pull out more greatness than has been experienced to that point. There is also the need to engage in better strategies of profiling the opponent and the performance environment. In these three pillars of understanding (the self, the opponent, the performance environment) there are lots of little nooks and crannies to look into.

When you land your first big win in life, enjoy that moment. Then, at a certain point shortly thereafter you need to look beyond the first win and consider where you want to go next. There is always a new place to go in terms of position. There is also a new place to go in how you execute your skills. The evolutions you can achieve are only impeded by the scope of your own vision. Success is not a time to sit back and rest on your laurels. Rather, it is a time to rejoice in your capacities and really search for methods to augment them.

Looking for New Layers

Great performers see themselves as onions with many layers of good substance. As the champion reaches inward, he looks to peel a layer of himself off and move closer to his very potential. His antithesis is the champion on paper who rides the wave of success without digging deeper into his capacities. Far too often, paper champions get caught up holding onto what they've already achieved, without developing new skills.

Great boxers need to let go of the shoreline and play in deep waters to really learn how to swim. The waves are bigger, and so the champion learns how to really swim. For the last four years I have devoted some of my research activity to uncovering how great champions continue to adapt from one level of greatness to the next. The consistent trend is the previously mentioned types of understanding (self, opponent, environment) and then taking the next step and gaining the skills to exert control at a newly discovered next level of performance.

At this very moment, as I write this page, I am out of my home country working with a king among kings. He is the unequivocal big dog in his weight division, worldwide. There are only five such boxers in the world today, and he is one of them! As we prepare for his next opponent, another great athlete, we are building in new layers to his training, to his fight week strategies, and also to his protocols for fight night. My client understands where he needs to go and is moving with his team in tandem toward greater performance.

A person's first instinct is always safety first. We like to protect what we have. We will guard our possessions with care and fight to protect them. When a dog chews on a bone and sees a larger one in his or her sightline, he has to let go of the smaller bone in order to lock down on a bigger, meatier one. There is always a bigger bone to be had and there also comes a time when if a dog continues to chew on the same bone, nothing remains, not even its marrow.

When it comes time to jump and move to the next level, you need to let go of the guardrail, and throw your body in the air. For a split second you might be suspended with no part of your body hanging onto something. There comes many a time in every person's life when it is time to let go, jump, and move to the next rung in the ladder. Do not set anchor at a level where you short-sell yourself and block your evolution. Evolving people are happy people, who are alive to their very core.

Packaging and Promotion

To this point it has been suggested the substance of a champion, in terms of performance output, is most important. However, gift-wrapping is also an important piece of the performer's packaging. There needs to be a certain mystique surrounding the identity of the champion. The champion's image can win him battles, just as his physical and psychological preparation will. Mystique is one more layer to the added depth of the king.

Mystique, meaning an untouchable image, is not something that just happens. It needs to be carefully crafted and marketed through impression management. Champions can remain champions for a very long time when the aura built around them suggests invincibility and fortitude. The champion cannot develop his image alone. He needs to work carefully with his management team and decide what exactly the message should be for public consumption. Part of his constitution might be built around tidiness, part around focus, and part around a level of preparation and knowledge that cannot be matched on the field of battle. With these messages combined, anyone wishing to profile the champion will soon realize he has far too much depth to be matched. There are some who are more equal than others.

Your goal when rising to the top is to build an image and projection that suggests you impenetrable. Part of how you go about featuring your strengths is by first understanding yourself and what you bring to the proverbial table. The rest of the task is about getting that information out through the correct channels. Your voice needs to be heard by the correct audience. As you gain opportunities to speak to your intended audience through targeted approaches, you need to keep in the back of your mind the words you share are more than just words. Each word and catch phrase needs to be viewed as part of who you wish to be in the eyes of the public. Half the battle is gaining access to your intended audience. The second part of the strategy requires you to understand, in advance, the message you wish to relay and how it ties back to where you are going.

REMINDERS FROM YOUR CORNER

- Great champions have a thirst for knowledge that remains especially where others would regard themselves as having “made it”. Success is a relative term and there is always another level of greatness to pursue.
- Each performer has multiple layers of greatness. When you think you’ve reached the best of yourself, consider this: if you were to have another layer of depth, what would it be?
- There is more to success than what you do. You need to build an image that features you to your targeted audience with an intended message. Your message should create fan interest and also an image of you that should enhance your performance and strike fear and doubt in your opponents.

Step Fifteen: Title Unifications

There comes a time when a champion needs to set sight on a worthy adversary. In the world of professional boxing, there could be upward of four or more world champions per weight division. The most confident champions look to accumulate championship belts and unifying titles. For the most capable of champions, the objective is to be a champion who unifies world titles. The unified world champion is the king among kings.

Unifications are not for the faint of heart and few world champions seek to go after additional titles immediately after the first big win. Instead, in the short-term, they look to defend their current title, gain experience as a world champion and build a winning record at the top. The thing about confidence is that it's built in layers, one layer upon another. The decision to go after an equal champion requires great timing and an understanding that at a certain point, to progress as a world champion, one must be prepared to risk it all and go after an additional world title. It is time to expand one's geography and conquer another king.

There will be a time in your life when you are at the top of your game. Some will believe that you've made it. As I mentioned in the last chapter, making it is a relative term: there is always more success to be gained if you have established skills to stand on. Far too often people stay within their own little ponds as big fish, protecting what they already have. At a certain point such people self-handicap by refusing to challenge themselves beyond their current level of accomplishment. Inside, such people know they are cheating themselves and creating a glass ceiling. Eventually the person who only looks to protect what he or she already has declines in ability, primarily because there is nothing more to achieve in one's current position – one begins to stand still. In this chapter, we consider how a champion can correctly conquer new territory and become the champion among champions.

Targeting Another Champion

A few months ago I worked with a client as part of a working team. We targeted another king, one the odds makers thought was far and away a better boxer than my client. Even though the odds in Las Vegas were 4:1 against us, we knew something that the odds makers didn't. Champions have times when they are untouchable and also times when they become vulnerable. The champion we targeted was on the pound for pound listing as among the five best boxers in the world across all of the weight divisions. However, his last several opponents were much older men and so, the pound for pounder was soft, his record was inflated, and so, he was over-rated.

The week of the fight arrived and from good solid profiling, we knew exactly where to go with our messages to the media and through press conferences and blogs. The adversary had a history of not trusting his management, evidenced through contract holdouts. He also changed coaches several times, again reflecting his lack of trust in those around him. All we needed to do was present our king as one perched on more solid ground. My client had worked with every member of his working team from his beginning in the sport and we all grew up together. He claimed in the press conferences that ensued that his success was built with stability in his team, in contrast to the other champion. Then, when the two were placed on the same stage, my client always took center stage and obscured his adversary. Before long the adversary retreated into himself in the press conference, then in the weigh-in, and finally during the fight. The rest was history! Even big kings can fall.

There are always several champions in play at one time. Once you are among them and you wish to expand your territory, choose your opponents wisely. Champions can be at the top of their game, fresh and sharp. There are times when champions also coast. As a motivational consultant I pride myself and fellow working team members in our ability to hand pick adversaries who are soft and vulnerable. You need to do the same. Target opportunities where people are coasting in success and then with both elbows at the ready make space and broaden your territory by taking down another king.

Staying Within

By the time a world champion looks to expand territory, there is a strong sense of self-awareness. Great champions learn new things about themselves all the time, even when they are at the top of their game. There are always new nooks and crannies to look in and deepen self-understanding.

Recently I have been working with a world champion at the very top echelon of boxing. He fights regularly on HBO for large amounts of money.

Ramping up for a recent fight the working team expected me to provide my traditional working profile of the champion's opponent – also a great champion in his own right.

Instead of providing a profile of the opponent, I did something that took the team by surprise. I profiled our champion and looked over his last six high profile fights for aspects that were perfectly executed such as a good press conference, weigh-in, media management, dressing room management, walk to the ring, touching of gloves, etc. Having analyzed all aspects of each performance I developed a performance plan that brought all of the good aspects together into one ultimate plan for the fight.

The fear when a promising champion comes up against another great champion is that he will forget what works for him or at very least, not package all that works for him into one comprehensive performance plan.

To be a unified world champion, one needs to do much more than just target a vulnerable champion; one also needs to bring one's "A Game" to the table. My objective was to work with my client and the working team on what we do best and then to focus exclusively on our own business while ramping up for the fight.

Sooner or later you will come up against an opponent who will attempt to win through gamesmanship. I will confess that by profiling an opponent and then handpicking vulnerable adversaries, my team and I have been known to play games, but never at the expense of our own focus.

No matter who is in front of you and how eminent the opponent, you can beat the best of the best by simply noticing only what matters: you and your working team. By staying inside of yourself and your team, indirectly you can floor people who try to entice you into games where you become the hunted. A good performer requires a thick shell and the conviction to stay within her/himself.

Lineal Champion

The ultimate objective for every world-class performer is to be the champion of champions, meaning top dog. In professional boxing, we call such people "lineal champions". These champions go one step beyond looking to unite titles by bumping off another champion in his weight division.

To be a lineal world champion, a boxer must compete and best the number one opponent in his weight division. In essence, he has to beat the best to be the best. Few boxers seek out the toughest of adversaries despite the inherent mythology surrounding boxing: that all boxers are warriors.

In terms of a world-class fighter's progression, becoming the lineal champion happens only after a world champion is ready to take on the best in the division and prove himself as the very best. As you might recall, there are many champions who don't dare perform against people at least as good as they are. Then again, the boxers who target lineal titles are not among the faint of heart. They are built of solid stock and have that special determination to be at the pinnacle of their domain. They are also the polar opposite to risk aversive – they like to take calculated chances. Calling out an equal happens when one is at the top of one's game with solid experience to stand, matched with a good dose of self-confidence, and not before.

In your life you will have the opportunity to fight for at least several world championship equivalents. At a certain point you will need to go "all in", at the very moment when you are at the top of your game. Becoming a lineal champion is as much about timing as it is about preparation. There is a certain time to jump forward and unify titles, and then another moment where you need to go beyond that point and jump upward, once more.

Life is all about jumping, leaving the ground and trusting that your feet will land on solid ground. Just as the best boxers need to jump at specific moments in their career, so too do you!

Not all people have the stomach to push themselves out of the comfort zone several times and move from one level to the next. The again, how might one ever know one's capabilities when there is no pushing and discomfort? The short answer is that discomfort is a good thing and people should push themselves out of the comfort zone regularly, even when they are champions in small to mid-sized ponds.

Discomfort is actually your friend! It will guide you toward progress and ensure that you don't sit back and rest on your laurels. There are always opportunities for warriors who seek them out. You need to dare yourself, unify titles, push your boundaries and eventually challenge to be the gold standard in your profession. Doing otherwise is to rob yourself of your God given talents.

REMINDERS FROM YOUR CORNER

- There comes a time when you need to step things up and compete against tough opponents. Target your high-end opponents wisely and if possible, identify those most vulnerable.
- Internal focus is the most important strategy when facing off against another champion. Stay within yourself no matter what.
- There will come a time when you should really challenge yourself and go up against the best people in your field. Instead of shying away from the possibility, once you are a champion on solid footing, with a few epic battles under your belt, make the leap and challenge the best of the best.
- Levels of success are not places you drop in anchor in, they are only stepping-stones to new and more challenging worlds.

Step Sixteen: The Champion in You

As you can see, there is a lot to be learned from the pinnacle of professional boxing. Boxing is a metaphor that matches up nicely with many of the challenges you experience daily. Some of those challenges happen in your workplace where you must compete against opponents, impress employers and look within yourself for answers and daily motivation.

There is no mistaking the perfect parallel between boxing and life. There are days when you are hit with a low blow, and times when you are up against the ropes. There are also moments in life that are the equivalent of championship rounds. Finally, there comes a time when you need to look beyond the borders of your accomplishments and seek out tougher challenges against the best of the best.

Every chapter in this book addresses one step that will propel you forward to contender, champion and then lineal champion's status. There is a high level warrior in you, just waiting to get out. The commitment to each progressive step requires time, desire and persistence on your part. There are many people out there in the world today to compete against and best. The people who make it to the top must set their sight on excellence and then go after what they dream about with a purpose, each and every day.

The good news is that many people choose not to compete at the elite level and become champions. Look around you in your workplace and you will find that people with desire and work ethic are few and far between. Most people are looking for security and stability, not championship status. The minute people look for stability, they are looking to protect what they have and automatically, their vision becomes short and constrained. You need to be different! Your vision needs to be endless, much like the skilled and well-guided contender. Boundaries are meant to be broken and glass ceilings are meant to be shattered.

What follows next are a few parting reminders that you need to keep in the forefront of your mind as you prepare to engage in battle. These suggestions are general, though also a crucial part of what will bring you to the next level and onward to victory.

KNOW YOURSELF

The starting point to excellence is self-awareness. Every great performer has a profound understanding of self. The wonderful thing about self-awareness is that it is a journey and not a destination. I have worked with many successful and accomplished athletes over the last twenty years. When I began working with each one of these performers it was obvious they knew quite a bit about what made them tick. Elite performers know generally what sits well in terms of diet and how to focus before an important performance.

My selling point was that I would help the client "pick up the crumbs", no matter how small. Great performances are built from lots of small crumbs that together gel into a performance strategy. All I had to do was go through a few memorable successful performances and look for patterns in terms of daily structure and also in terms of tactics. The minute we discovered one small crumb the athlete was not aware of, and using by accident, we spoke about how to intentionally integrate that aspect within her/his performance plan.

Even as I am presently working with a lineal champion, my job is to push the champion forward in his self-awareness. Understanding of the self is much like an onion, with many layers. When you peel back one layer of the onion, you learn something new about yourself. Unlike an onion, though, the layers of self-awareness and the possibilities for self-discovery are endless. There is always something new to discover about your self.

To develop, you need to look within and constantly identify new insights. The minute you engage in self-knowledge you mobilize your focus and at the same time you invest in your future. It is one thing to understand your opponent, but first, you need to understand who you are and why you perform the way you do. Performance is a systematic process where good decisions need to be made and parceled together every day. Imagine if more people understood what made them tick and then proceeded into every day of work with a comprehensive performance plan? The workplace would indeed be a very exciting place to be!

Your commitment to excellence must be ongoing. Each day you need to evaluate your performance and discover the lessons that are there to be gained.

Many of the people around you are grossly inefficient. They make the same mistakes over and over again. When sloppy people make good decisions, far too often those decisions are random efforts, either never to be repeated again, or efforts repeated from time to time without consistency. Great performers have more than just natural ability. They also have the skills to perform with excellence regardless of their mood or the day's circumstances. Greatness is something that is produced and improved upon from one day to the next. Over time, if you engage in an approach where excellence is always the focus, few will ever be able to keep pace. You will become the leader and lineal world champion through great decisions, based upon profound self-awareness. Excellence starts with what you do systematically each day.

Dare to keep a logbook and document your daily performance. When you have a particularly good day, take a look at the activities you did, your decisions, your mood, your amount of rest, nutrition, and hydration. Also look at your social exchanges experienced that day. See if you could gain one crumb with each entry. Then, at the very end of every month, go through that month's logbook with a colored pen and underline new insights. At the back of the logbook set aside no more than the last two pages as the summary points that comprise your performance plan.

Know Your Opponent

Just as it is important to understand what makes you tick, so too is it necessary to understand your opponent. Sun Tzu was known to say: "wars are won before they are ever fought". From what we have discussed in this book, you and I would be inclined to agree. Even when you fully understand yourself, no one performs in isolation. There are challenges that come from the environment, in the form of commitments and adversaries. In terms of your adversaries, you need to understand who you are competing against in order to best these people.

Opponents have tendencies, strengths and weaknesses. You need to fully engage in solid research processes to gain a detailed appreciation of what makes your opponent tick. Far too often people only gain a superficial understanding of their opponents through intuition, word of mouth and some observation. Though all of the above are important parts of how you learn about your opponent, I suggest a much more systematic approach to your research. Opponents need to be attacked on their weak side. You need to fully understand what your opponent's weaknesses are and equally, why a weakness is a weakness. The depth of your knowledge will then win you many battles that you could not win based on personal skills and self-knowledge, alone.

Before you enter into battle, allocate at least one full week to fully understand your potential employer, or some other adversary that you are about to encounter. Know every little detail about that person, gained through media outlets, social networking pages, online curriculum vitas, and personal and organizational web pages. Next, once you know what needs to be known about the opponent, set aside at least a few days to really memorize and understand your opponent. You need all of the information you have gained at your fingertips when the time comes to engage in battle.

A Quality Team

Every great champion develops and then remains a champion partly as a result of the people he surrounds himself with. In professional boxing, many great champions have been torn down by either not choosing a good team from the beginning or dismantling their quality team and replacing it with people who lacked character and did not have the athlete's best interest at heart. Talent and discipline are important pieces to the performer's package and they cannot be cultivated in a poor performance environment.

When you decide to go after champion's status, you need to look beyond yourself to the people you choose to surround yourself with. Your selection of working team members should be comprised of people with: (a) knowledge, (b) a history of affiliation with success, (c) character, and (d) the capacity to work as part of the team. It is easy enough to find members of a working team, but when you select your team, make certain that each and every member has all four core characteristics. If there are deficits in any of the above areas in a prospective working team member, that deficit will only become larger as you come closer to championship status, or go deeper into bout preparation.

Once you have selected your team, you then need to build a positive history with each member and the team as a whole. It is one thing to construct a good working team and an entirely other thing to maintain and enhance its composition over the long-term. Good relationships can become soured through neglect, a lack of recognition, and poor communication. You need to continue to invest in your team and its members each and every day. Though money is a motivator, at a certain point, so too is the relationship and trust you have forged with each member. Investing in your members serves as a double-dividend. As you work to support them, you are only further supporting yourself.

Your task, then, is to go about identifying the members for your team. Once you have chosen the best members you can, work with them and invest your time generously. No matter what, allocate time to each member, as the team is comprised of individual members with personalities, life stories, and uniqueness. You need to learn about each member, get to know him or her well, and then continue to weave each member into the team as a valuable part of a larger whole. Though some people like to take short cuts and trade up to better teams, remember that good teams are built through long-standing history and "time invested" in the uphill climb.

Eyes on the Prize

The path to championship status requires lots of effort and an investment of time. From the point you embark on a career or a trajectory of your life where you are targeting the top, you can expect that it will take several years to reach the summit. There is an entire area of research termed "expertise" where it has been found that to become an expert in any aspect of life, one requires a commitment of ten years and ten thousand hours of focused investment.

With a journey to the top that requires time and a daily investment of energy, it sometimes becomes a challenge to persist. People become fatigued by the daily grind of life and repetitive practice in the workplace. There are more fatigued than energized people in every achievement setting. Your challenge is to retain your energy and enthusiasm where others won't. After all, you need to bring your "A Game" with you each and every day, not just on select days and during fleeting moments.

With the challenge of mobilizing effort, you will be faced with how to bring the best of yourself forward, consistently. Those who make it to the top in any area of achievement do exactly that! Every morning they wake up and decide what they will achieve on that day and look at how that day's decisions will bring them closer to an overarching goal of long-term success. People who eventually make it to the summit always keep their eyes on the prize. They work with a purpose and take baby steps forward each and every day.

My suggestion is that each morning when you wake-up, take five minutes to yourself and decide what you would like to achieve that day. You need also to consider the approach you are going to take in the achievement setting and how you will build energy through the day despite any challenges you might encounter. When I work with professional boxers, I always ask them to post one copy of their goals on the wall by their bed, with a second copy at their work desk. Many also post additional copies of their goals in the most frequented placed they go each day, including the refrigerator. You need to read your goals each and every day, many times. We all focus on something. Your focus needs to be directed toward where you are going; nowhere else.

Close the Show

There will also come a time where you are so close to your objectives that you could almost touch them. Many performers close the distance between their dreams and reality and finally reach the level they need to perform at to become champions. In that very moment when they could close the show they make poor decisions that self-sabotage, re-creating distance between where they are and where they need to go. The underlying barriers in the final few yards, many times, reflect either a fear of failure or a fear of success.

Few are the people in the final steps before becoming champions who don't question whether they have what it takes to close the show. After so many hours, days and years of emotional and time investment it stands to reason that one needs to produce the goods. Without pressure most everyone can succeed. What makes a champion different from others is that she or he produces a quality performance regardless of how high the expectations in one's environment. The focus is not on just on where the contender came from, but instead, where the journey will take him or her next.

Closing the show, or sealing the deal, is a necessary part of what you need to do. Moments will come, when mark my words the opponent's jugular will be exposed. The opponent at a certain point will become vulnerable to what you are selling. At that very moment, you need to pounce on your opportunities, take the necessary step forward and move in for the kill.

When I work with people in the final few days before they become champions we only focus on the days ahead. We never consider all of the surrounding expectations that might or might not result in the future. The focus is to live in the present, narrow one's focus and target only the challenge immediately in front of the contender. As the saying goes: "one step at a time".

Then the moment comes within the performance when you will need to step up and produce a champion's effort. At that moment, you will step into the light, push your opponent backward and close the distance to greatness.

You will need to remain in the present, focused only on the performance, and not on what that performance might mean. You will need to perform from the sound of the first bell through the sounding of the final bell. Every second along the way you will need to put forward maximum effort, and nothing less. Becoming a champion requires maximum effort through to the final accomplishment of your performance. Where others typically are not attentive, you need to be in the present moment and second to close the show.

Extend Greatness

There will come a time when you will become a champion. If you follow the sixteen steps I have armed you with in this book, it is only a matter of when. Some would say that becoming a champion is one thing, remaining a champion is another. If you look at many of the performers who rise to the top in their fields, you will indeed see that some can make it, but that most have very short tenures at the top.

Far too often, people train to become champions and then forget to re-focus their objectives after the fact. It is one thing to be great for a short period of time, for a fleeting moment. High achievers look at their momentary greatness and wish to experience other such moments, again and again. Many an Olympic Champion qualifies and then returns for a second Olympics in order to gain that second Gold Medal. Though on paper, these people are already Olympic Champions, they see within themselves the potential for better things to come. These select few look to refine their skills to the next level and extend their reign at the top.

You need to push yourself out of the comfort zone, even when you become a champion. There are many layers of achievement open to you and when you first become a champion, you experience only the first moment of potentially, many such moments. The thing about great champions is that they look to expand their territory and always consider where they wish to go next, once they achieve a new level of greatness. There are always new lands to conquer.

Your task is to be proactive, much as any great champion would be. You need to go after your dreams while they are fresh and within your grasp. There will be moments at each level of greatness and you should enjoy each one. There will also be moments when you need to jump with both feet to the next level of performance. Dare to be different and "let go" of your current level of greatness so that you might bring your game to the next level. Even if at a certain point you do not achieve an objective, there is something noble in having tried for better. Also, you will be the antithesis to those soured by regret after the fact. There are enough of these sorts of regretful people in the world around you.

REMINDERS FROM YOUR CORNER

- You need to know exactly what makes you tick. Every person knows intuitively how to perform at a reasonable level. To be a champion, however, you need to be far more systematic.
- You need to be equally systematic when your profile your opponents. Every person is gifted with certain instincts and blink impressions used to profile opponents. You need to go beyond your instincts and intuition and understand your opponent.
- When you step into the trenches each day, there will be times when you will feel emotionally flat or fatigued. Your challenge is to keep your eyes on the prize and continue to advance, with small steps each and every day.
- There will also come a moment when you will have that championship ring in your grasp. When the championship is within your reach, you need to step forward, remain focused in the present, bump out the previous champion, and take what is yours.
- When you finally become champion, enjoy the moment for a little while, but not too long. Your championship title reflects one moment of greatness. You are capable of having several great moments, so dare to re-set your goals and expand your territory. People are often only limited by the scope of their vision.

Conclusion

Robert Schinke has consulted with professional boxers who are world champions since 2001. His clients have achieved the highest echelon of athletic performance, winning championships performances featured on HBO and ShowTime. In this book, Dr. Schinke, an internationally celebrated Canada Research Chair in Multicultural Sport, a university sport psychology professor, and nationally registered motivational coach,offers sixteen chronological steps from the world of elite professional boxing to bring you to the championship level in your work performance. Lessons include how to become more self-aware, how to work within a team environment, how to profile an opponent, hot to prepare for battle, how to systematically deliver a championship performance, and how to analyze and learn from previous experiences.

From the book, you, much like the world championship boxer, will exceed your potential and become a performer to contend with. The skills you gain from this book will formalize you as a championship performer with a systematic approach for battle preparation and delivery.Each chapter is authored as a condensed installment with summary points. This book is written for professionals striving to perform in the workplace. The metaphors and lessons borrowed from the elite boxing world are provided to the reader in an easily accessible series of steps.

INDEX

D

E

F

G

H

I

K

L